SKINNY CHOCOLATE

SKINNY CHOCOLATE

PHYLLIS MAGIDA
BARBARA GRUNES

Surrey Books

Chicago

SKINNY CHOCOLATE is published by Surrey Books, Inc., 230 E. Ohio St., Suite 120, Chicago, IL 60611.

First edition: 1 2 3 4 5

This book is manufactured in the United States of America.

Library of Congress Cataloging-in-Publication data:

Magida, Phyllis.
    Skinny chocolate / by Phyllis Magida and Barbara Grunes.
        210 p.   cm.
    Includes index.
    ISBN 0-940625-80-6 (pbk.) : $12.95
    1. Low-fat diet—Recipes. 2. Cookery (Chocolate) 3. Reducing diets—Recipes. I. Grunes, Barbara. II. Title.
    RM237.7.M34   1994
    641.8'65—dc20   93-44577
                                                   CIP

Editorial and production: *Bookcrafters, Inc., Chicago*
Art Director: *Hughes & Co., Chicago*
Nutritional analyses: *Linda R. Yoakum, M.S., R.D.*
Cover and interior illustrations by *Laurel DiGangi*
Back cover photos courtesy Chocolate Manufacturers Association

For free catalog and prices on quantity purchases, contact Surrey Books at the address above.

This title is distributed to the trade by Publishers Group West.

Other titles in the "Skinny" Cookbooks Series:

Skinny Beef
Skinny Chicken
Skinny Cookies, Cakes & Sweets
Skinny One-Pot Meals
Skinny Pasta
Skinny Pizzas

Skinny Potatoes
Skinny Sauces
Skinny Seafood
Skinny Soups
Skinny Spices

CONTENTS

FOREWORD

Look at the chocolate recipes of the '50s and you'll actually be startled. By today's standards, they seem to be designed at the breaking point of richness, with as many and much calories, fat, and cholesterol as can be mixed into a batter.

But today's chocolate recipe requirements are as different as the people who eat them. Chocolate lovers of the '90s exercise and watch their fat, calorie, sodium, and cholesterol intake. They search out chocolate dishes that are simultaneously healthy and delicious.

Well, here they are—over 100 "skinny chocolate" recipes. And we're genuinely proud of each and every one. For months now we've dreamed chocolate, thought chocolate, talked chocolate, and bought chocolate. We've cooked with it, longed for it when we weren't eating it, and savored it when we were.

We've tested, tasted, and adapted classics from several continents. We've modified personal favorites and created dishes we think will become your favorites.

We've walked around with smudged mouths and fingers and become very popular with the children in the neighborhood.

But despite our chocoholic behavior, *neither of us has gained a pound.* The reason, of course, is that the recipes in this book are even skinnier and healthier than we thought possible when we began to work on them.

To control fat and calories, we've used every trick in a chocolate lover's handbook, from aspartame sweetener and whipped topping mix to fructose sugar, chocolate extract, and evaporated skim milk. We've used no-fat yogurt and no-fat sour cream rather than traditional products. And we've used ricotta cheese and 1% cottage cheese instead of regular cottage cheese.

We've rediscovered ingredients like gelatin, too. And we've explored a few out-of-the-mainstream foodstuffs, such as tofu and carob. We've used non-stick sprays and diet margarine rather than whole margarine; and we've replaced egg yolks with real egg substitute.

Before we began this book, we admitted to a prejudice against cocoa as a replacement for chocolate. But after using cocoa in myriad ways, our prejudice has undergone a 180-degree change: we're now prejudiced in *favor* of it rather than against it.

We've even included a mini-primer of "skinny ingredients," describing some of the new and less familiar ingredients we call for in this book.

Despite our changes and substitutions, our replacements and reductions, we've never sacrificed flavor. When a recipe met our stringent diet requirements but just didn't taste good enough, we dumped it in the disposer and went back to the kitchen.

Our recipes range in intensity from chocolate mousse, with its rich and intense flavor, to chocolate pumpkin pudding, in which the chocolate taste is so faint and delicate that it functions as an enhancement, an undertaste to the classic dish.

What you have here are the best "skinny chocolate" recipes we could develop. We hope you enjoy making and eating them as much as we enjoyed creating them for you.

Phyllis Magida and Barbara Grunes

SKINNY INGREDIENTS PRIMER

We've looked at numerous cookbooks pretending to be healthier and lower in calories, but in too many cases the recipes turned out to be the same as those found in any other cookbook except that the dish was cut into smaller portions. Our recipes, however, are the "real thing": chocolate foods that contain little or no fat and cholesterol and are reduced in calories. We were able to do this for one reason: "skinny" ingredients.

Not only did we take advantage of such time-honored substitutions as cocoa for chocolate and whipped topping for whipped cream; but we also used many new reduced-calorie and low- or non-fat ingredients such as no-fat sour cream and real egg substitute. Thanks to these and similar foods, we were able to write what we think is a bona fide "skinny chocolate" recipe book.

Because some of the ingredients may be unfamiliar, we're including this little primer—a description of these foods that we hope you'll find useful.

♦ *Aspartame Sweetener* Made of food components found in meat, fruit, and milk, this almost-no-calorie sweetener can be used in any non-baked product or even in a baked product provided it's added after baking. Aspartame sweetener is available in bulk, and a sugar equivalency table is printed on the package.

♦ *Carob Powder* Made from the naturally sweet, starchy pod of a tree native to Syria, this powder's flavor, many feel, is a satisfactory, if bland, substitute for cocoa and chocolate. Carob powder contains about 14 calories and 0.04 grams of fat per tablespoon, as compared to cocoa's 10.6 calories and 0.5 gram of fat.

♦ *Chocolate Extract* A cocoa-based extract that enhances chocolate flavor when added in small amounts. It's available at supermarkets.

♦ *Cocoa and Dutch Cocoa* Sometimes cocoa is processed with an alkaline ingredient, which reduces the acid in the cocoa. This processing gives it a darker appearance and a mellower flavor. Cocoa processed this way is called Dutch cocoa. Some Dutch cocoa manufacturers insist that Dutch cocoa can be used interchangeably with regular cocoa. But we think that adding an equivalent amount of Dutch cocoa results in a dish that's a little too chocolatey for most tastes. So when substituting Dutch for regular cocoa, we always reduce the amount of Dutch cocoa slightly.

One tablespoon of cocoa contains about 10.6 calories and 0.5 gram of fat. A tablespoon (½ ounce) of unsweetened chocolate, however, contains 70 calories and 7.5 grams of fat.

When cocoa is substituted for chocolate in a recipe, the standard is usually 3 tablespoons of cocoa along with a few teaspoons of fat for each ounce of chocolate called for. But we've found that this exchange is unreliable; there is no rule of thumb, and substitutions must be done on an individual basis.

There are several ways to add cocoa to recipes:
1. When the recipe involves flour, the cocoa can be sifted with the flour and added to the batter at the same time.
2. Cocoa can be combined with a liquid and stirred with a whisk until a very smooth paste results, which can then be added to the recipe.
3. If the recipe involves processing in a food processor or pureeing in a blender, the cocoa can be added to the ingredients being processed or blended.

♦ *Diet Margarine* Depending on the manufacturer, the same product may be described as diet, light, or extra-light margarine. The stick margarine used to develop these recipes contained 5.7 grams of fat per tablespoon and 50 calories, as compared to regular margarine, which contains 11.4 grams of fat and 101 calories. Although the manufacturer does not recommend it for baking, we used diet margarine in several recipes with excellent results.

♦ *Egg White Whipping*   Since so many recipes in this book involve whipping whites and folding meringues into batters, we decided to include these instructions for whipping large numbers of egg whites.
1. Use fresh eggs to get maximum volume.
2. Although egg whites are supposed to whip better (to a larger volume) by hand in a copper bowl, we know of no one personally who ever does this since the effort of whipping by hand far outweighs the benefits of larger volume. If you must have more volume, add another egg white, and whip your whites in the electric mixer.
3. Whip egg whites at room temperature.
4. When whipping egg whites to fold into batters, add sugar to make them into a meringue. Meringues are much heartier than plain whipped egg whites and will hold their volume better throughout the folding process.
5. To whip egg whites, begin at low speed. This will create small air bubbles (high speed produces large bubbles that aren't as stable as small ones). As soon as the egg whites begin to hold soft peaks (peaks whose tips fall over when beaters are lifted from the foam), add cream of tartar. This ingredient will help stabilize the air bubbles.
6. Continue beating at low speed until whites begin to hold stiff peaks (peaks whose tips do not fall over when beaters are lifted from the foam). At this point, increase speed to medium and beat until foam holds good, stiff peaks.
7. With beaters running, add sugar in a thin stream. As soon as sugar has been added, turn off beaters.

♦ *Fructose Sugar*   Regular table sugar is an ingredient known to scientists as a disaccharide, a type of carbohydrate that combines two simple sugars, glucose and fructose. Both are sweeteners and contain the same calories per tablespoon (48) and the same fat content (0).

The main difference between the two is that fructose, or fruit sugar, is sweeter, so if used alone, a smaller amount is needed. Hence, many of our recipes call for fructose. Although fructose product labels claim that if used as a substitute for table sugar, the amount of sugar in a recipe can be reduced by one-fourth to one-third, we found this too variable to be a rule.

Fructose sugar is available at most supermarkets in either the baking or diet section. If fructose is not available, you can substitute regular table sugar in any recipe, increasing slightly—and to taste—the quantity called for.

In recipes that just call for "sugar," simply use regular table sugar. If you wish to substitute fructose sugar for regular table sugar in a recipe, follow the instructions on the package, but use as little fructose as possible and then taste the batter. If you want the dish sweeter, add more fructose before putting the dish in the oven.

♦ *No-Fat Cream Cheese*   Described on the label as "Non-fat Pasteurized Process Cream Cheese Product," this ingredient has 25 calories per ounce and 0 grams of fat, as compared to about 100 calories and 10 grams of fat in regular cream cheese.

The manufacturer recommends it for spreading and non-baked recipes; because of its softer consistency, it's not suggested for baking.

Nevertheless, we use it as a primary ingredient in some of our recipes. In our cheesecake, for example, the cake was delicious but the soft texture of the non-fat cream cheese caused several splits in the cake top, which we masked successfully with a meringue.

♦ *No-Fat Ricotta Cheese*   This soft, unripened fresh cheese, smoother than cottage cheese, is made from the whey of mozzarella with the fat removed. No-fat ricotta contains about 11 calories and 0 grams of fat per tablespoon, as compared to 25 calories and almost 2 grams of fat in part-skim ricotta.

♦ *No-Fat Sour Cream*   Described on the label as "Real Dairy No-Fat Sour Cream," this ingredient has 15 calories per ounce and 0 grams of fat, as compared to the 62 calories and 6 grams of fat in regular sour cream.

We found it a perfect substitute for regular sour cream in both baked and unbaked recipes. There are several brands on the market and some look and taste much better than others; so if you find one you don't like, simply buy another brand.

♦ *No-Fat Yogurt*   Made from curdled skim milk, this thick semi-solid bacterial culture contains 7.5 calories and 0 grams of fat per tablespoon, as compared to 9 calories and .22 grams of fat in low-fat yogurt.

♦ *1% Cottage Cheese*   Cottage cheese is available with varying amounts of fat, ranging from no-fat to 1%, 2%, and 4% fat. We chose to use the 1% cottage cheese in this book. A tablespoon of 1% cottage cheese contains 0.14 grams of fat and 10.25 calories, as compared to regular (4%) cottage cheese, which contains 0.63 grams of fat and 14.5 calories.

♦ *Real Egg Substitute*   (liquid) Often described on the label as containing zero fat and cholesterol, this product, a pasteurized blend of egg whites and other ingredients, substitutes well for whole eggs in baked recipes.

Package instructions usually say to use ¼ cup real egg substitute for each whole egg called for. Calories vary from 25 to 40 and fat varies from 0 to about 6.5 grams per quarter cup. Cholesterol varies from 0 to about 1 milligram.

Compare this to a regular egg, which contains about 5 grams of fat, 75 calories, and 213 milligrams of cholesterol.

To substitute for egg yolks, simply measure out 1½ tablespoons of real egg substitute for each yolk called for. When a recipe calls for whites, use real egg whites and discard the yolks, which contain all the cholesterol and all the fat. An average-size egg white contains only 17 calories, 0 fat, and 0 cholesterol.

♦ *"Still" Freezing*   Even if you don't have an ice cream maker, you can still make frozen treats minus the ice crystals by the "still" freezing method. This method combines the refrigerator-freezer and food processor (or electric mixer) and is simple to do:

1. Combine ingredients as described in recipe, up to where they're to be processed in the ice cream maker.
2. Pour into metal bowl and cover well. Place in freezer for about 2 hours.
3. Next, process in food processor (if frozen solid, break into chunks before adding to processor). Or beat with electric mixer until well combined but not melted.
4. Place in serving bowl, cover well, and return to freezer until serving time.

♦ *Whipped Topping Mix* One manufacturer described this product as a dry mix containing sugar, tropical oils, and milk byproducts, among other ingredients. When combined with vanilla and cold milk and whipped, one envelope yields two cups of whipped topping, which substitutes well for whipped cream.

When combined with skim milk, one tablespoon of whipped topping contains 7.25 calories and 0 grams of fat, as compared to 15 calories and 1.6 grams of fat in regular whipped cream.

1.
CHOCOLATE CAKES

Chocolate Sponge Cake

Chocolate Sponge-Angel Cake

Soft Chocolate Sponge Cake

Chocolate Sponge Cake with Chocolate Apple Frosting

Casserole Sponge Cake with Chocolate Cottage Cheese Frosting

Chocolate Victorian Sandwich

Cake Roll with Whipped Cocoa-Banana Filling

Chocolate-Filled Cake Roll

Dutch Cocoa Roll

Cocoa Gingerbread Cake

Chocolate "Sour Cream" Cake

Fudge Cake with Cocoa Icing

Chocolate Cake with Pureed Prunes

Cocoa Tea Cake

Chocolate Tea Cake with Italian Meringue Frosting

Marble Cake

Peach Upside-Down Cake

CHOCOLATE SPONGE CAKE

Dutch processed cocoa has some of the acidity removed, and it gives a darker color when cooked. The process was developed in Holland, hence the name "Dutch" cocoa.

8 Servings

 2 egg whites
 ¾ cup fructose (fruit sugar, see p. 3), divided
 ½ teaspoon cream of tartar
 ½ cup real egg substitute
 2 tablespoons unsweetened Dutch cocoa
 ¾ cup water, room temperature
1½ cups all-purpose flour
 ¼ teaspoon salt

Preheat oven to 325° F. Use ungreased 10-inch tube pan.

In large bowl of electric mixer, beat egg whites until almost stiff. Sprinkle whites with ¼ cup fructose and cream of tartar. Continue beating until stiff, but not dry, peaks form. Set aside.

In clean bowl, add egg substitute. Mix cocoa with remaining fructose and add to bowl, blending ingredients together. Blend in water.

Sift flour and salt onto batter; fold with spatula to incorporate. Fold egg whites into batter.

Spoon into ungreased tube pan. Set on center rack in oven and bake 45 minutes or until a cake tester or bamboo skewer inserted in cake comes out dry.

Invert cake onto rack; allow to cool. Remove cake from pan and turn it right side up. Cool.

Nutritional Data

PER SERVING		EXCHANGES	
Calories:	153	Milk:	0.0
% Calories from fat:	2	Veg.:	0.0
Fat (gm):	0.4	Fruit:	1.0
Sat. fat (gm):	0.1	Bread:	1.0
Cholesterol (mg):	0	Meat:	0.5
Sodium (mg):	102	Fat:	0.5
Protein (gm):	5		
Carbohydrate (gm):	32		

CHOCOLATE SPONGE-ANGEL CAKE

This sponge is a soft cross between an angel food cake and a sponge cake.

12 Servings

- 9 tablespoons real egg substitute
- 1½ teaspoons vanilla
- 1 cup fructose (fruit sugar, see p. 3), divided
- 2 tablespoons unsweetened Dutch cocoa
- 1 cup cake flour, scant, sifted before measuring
- 1 teaspoon baking powder
- 6 large egg whites
- ¾ teaspoon cream of tartar
- Confectioners' sugar

P lace oven rack in center of oven and preheat oven to 350 degrees. In electric mixer bowl, beat egg substitute with vanilla until thick. Add ½ cup of fructose and beat again.

Combine cocoa, flour, and baking powder. With beaters running at low speed, add dry ingredients 2 tablespoons at a time until well mixed.

In separate bowl, beat egg whites until they hold soft peaks, add cream of tartar, and continue beating until they hold stiff peaks. With beaters running, add remaining ½ cup fructose in a thin stream. As soon as sugar is incorporated, turn off beaters.

Fold meringue into batter. Spoon batter into an ungreased, 10-inch tube pan. Bake 45 to 50 minutes or until top of cake springs back when touched lightly with fingertip.

Remove from oven, invert on wire rack and let cool thoroughly. Loosen cooled cake from sides of pan with a thin knife or spatula.

At serving time, place cake, right side up, on serving platter and sprinkle generously with confectioners' sugar. Use a serrated knife to cut cake into quarters. Cut each quarter into three pieces.

Nutritional Data

PER SERVING		EXCHANGES	
Calories:	98	Milk:	0.0
% Calories from fat:	2	Veg.:	0.0
Fat (gm):	0.2	Fruit:	0.0
Sat. fat (gm):	trace	Bread:	1.0
Cholesterol (mg):	0	Meat:	0.5
Sodium (mg):	71	Fat:	0.0
Protein (gm):	4		
Carbohydrate (gm):	20		

SOFT CHOCOLATE SPONGE CAKE

This cake is delicately chocolate. If you want a more intense chocolate taste, add a few drops of chocolate extract when you add the vanilla extract.

9 Servings

Non-stick cooking spray
1 cup cake flour, scant, sifted before measuring
1½ tablespoons unsweetened Dutch cocoa
1 teaspoon baking powder
⅓ cup real egg substitute
¾ teaspoon vanilla extract
8 tablespoons fructose (fruit sugar, see p. 3), divided
¼ cup skim milk
4 large egg whites
½ teaspoon cream of tartar
Confectioners' sugar

Adjust oven rack to center of oven and preheat oven to 350 degrees. Line a 9 x 9-inch-square cake pan on bottom with baking paper, and spray paper and pan sides with non-stick cooking spray.

Sift flour with cocoa and baking powder.

In electric mixer bowl, beat egg substitute with vanilla, chocolate extract if used, and 4 tablespoons fructose until very well mixed. Beat in flour/cocoa mixture; then beat in skim milk.

In separate bowl, beat egg whites until they hold soft peaks, add cream of tartar, and continue beating until they hold stiff peaks. With beaters running, add remaining 4 tablespoons fructose. As soon as sugar is incorporated, turn off beaters.

Fold meringue into batter.

Spoon batter into prepared pan. Bake 20 to 23 minutes or until cake tests done in center with bamboo skewer or cake tester. Remove from oven and invert onto wire rack to cool.

When cool, cut cake into 9 squares. Sprinkle liberally with confectioners' sugar before serving.

Nutritional Data

PER SERVING		EXCHANGES	
Calories:	93	Milk:	0.0
% Calories from fat:	2	Veg.:	0.0
Fat (gm):	0.2	Fruit:	0.0
Sat. fat (gm):	trace	Bread:	1.0
Cholesterol (mg):	0.1	Meat:	0.5
Sodium (mg):	77	Fat:	0.0
Protein (gm):	4		
Carbohydrate (gm):	19		

CHOCOLATE SPONGE CAKE WITH CHOCOLATE APPLE FROSTING

This cake is equally delicious with or without the frosting. If you serve it plain, add a sprinkling of confectioners' sugar. If you frost and have leftovers, cover cake and refrigerate. Cake will look and taste just as delicious the following day.

8 Servings

Non-stick cooking spray
9 tablespoons real egg substitute
1½ teaspoons vanilla
½ plus ⅓ cup fructose (fruit sugar, see p. 3), divided
1 tablespoon diet margarine, melted
15 tablespoons cake flour (1 cup less 1 tablespoon), sifted before measuring
2 tablespoons unsweetened Dutch cocoa
6 large egg whites
¾ teaspoon cream of tartar
Chocolate Apple Frosting (recipe follows)

Adjust oven rack to center of oven and preheat oven to 300 degrees. Coat a 9-inch springform pan with non-stick cooking spray.

In electric mixer bowl, beat egg substitute with vanilla until fluffy. Add ½ cup of fructose and beat again. Beat in margarine.

Sift flour and cocoa together and add to batter, beating until well combined.

In separate bowl, beat egg whites until they hold soft peaks; then beat in cream of tartar until they hold stiff peaks. With beaters running, add remaining ⅓ cup fructose in a thin stream. As soon as sugar is incorporated, turn off beaters.

Fold meringue into batter. Spoon batter into prepared springform pan.

Bake about 50 minutes or until cake tests done in center with bamboo skewer or cake tester. Remove from oven.

Carefully run a thin knife or spatula along sides of springform and remove sides. Leave cake on bottom of springform. Set on wire rack to cool.

When cool, use a serrated knife to cut cake in half horizontally. Transfer bottom layer to serving platter. Use a rubber spatula to cover bottom layer with ⅓ of Chocolate Apple Frosting. Place top layer over frosting. Cover sides with another ⅓ of frosting. Cover top with remaining frosting.

At serving time, cut cake into quarters; cut each quarter into 2 pieces.

Chocolate Apple Frosting
1 envelope whipped topping mix
4 teaspoons unsweetened Dutch cocoa
½ teaspoon vanilla extract
½ cup cold skim milk
1 cup peeled, chopped apple (use sweet apples, such as Macintosh)

Place whipped topping in electric mixer bowl along with cocoa, vanilla, and skim milk. Use a wire whisk to thoroughly combine ingredients. Beat according to package directions until frosting holds stiff peaks. Fold in chopped apple.

Nutritional Data

PER SERVING		EXCHANGES	
Calories:	171	Milk:	0.0
% Calories from fat:	6	Veg.:	0.0
Fat (gm):	1	Fruit:	0.5
Sat. fat (gm):	0.2	Bread:	2.0
Cholesterol (mg):	0.3	Meat:	0.0
Sodium (mg):	96	Fat:	0.0
Protein (gm):	6		
Carbohydrate (gm):	33		

CASSEROLE SPONGE CAKE WITH CHOCOLATE COTTAGE CHEESE FROSTING

♦

This cake is quickly made and large enough for a crowd.

♦

16 Servings

Non-stick cooking spray
⅔ cup real egg substitute
1 teaspoon vanilla extract
½ teaspoon almond extract
1 cup fructose (fruit sugar, see p. 3), divided
2 teaspoons baking powder
2 cups cake flour, scant, sifted before measuring
½ cup skim milk
8 large egg whites
1 teaspoon cream of tartar
Chocolate Cottage Cheese Frosting (recipe follows)
Confectioners' sugar

A djust oven rack to center of oven and preheat oven to 325 degrees. Line a 9 x 13-inch casserole on bottom with baking paper and spray paper and pan sides with non-stick cooking spray.

In electric mixer bowl, beat egg substitute with vanilla and almond extracts and ½ cup of fructose until well mixed.

Beat in baking powder. Add flour alternately with milk.

Beat egg whites until they hold soft peaks, add cream of tartar, and continue beating until they hold stiff peaks. With beaters running, add remaining ½ cup fructose. As soon as sugar is incorporated, turn beaters off.

Fold meringue into batter.

Spoon batter into prepared pan. Bake 25 to 28 minutes or until cake *just* tests done in center with bamboo skewer or cake tester. Do not overbake or cake will develop a tough crust.

Remove from oven and invert casserole on wire rack to cool. When cool, transfer cake to clean casserole and use a rubber spatula to spread Chocolate Cottage Cheese Frosting over top.

Cut cake into quarters; then cut each quarter into four pieces. Sprinkle frosting with confectioners' sugar before serving.

Chocolate Cottage Cheese Frosting

Makes ⅔ cup

- ½ cup 1% cottage cheese, drained in strainer
- 2 tablespoons diet margarine
- 2 teaspoons unsweetened Dutch cocoa
- 1 teaspoons aspartame sweetener
- ¼ teaspoon vanilla extract

Spoon cottage cheese into food processor or blender and process until smooth.

Add margarine, cocoa, aspartame, and vanilla. Process again until well combined. Use to frost top of Casserole Sponge Cake.

Nutritional Data

PER SERVING		EXCHANGES	
Calories:	116	Milk:	0.0
% Calories from fat:	8	Veg.:	0.0
Fat (gm):	1	Fruit:	0.0
Sat. fat (gm):	0.2	Bread:	1.5
Cholesterol (mg):	0.5	Meat:	0.0
Sodium (mg):	135	Fat:	0.0
Protein (gm):	5		
Carbohydrate (gm):	21		

CHOCOLATE VICTORIAN SANDWICH

The classic Victorian sandwich is made with two layers of white sponge cake sandwiched together with jam. We use a mild chocolate cake base and a low-calorie red raspberry spread, which makes it perfect for children.

16 Servings, 1 sandwich each

Non-stick cooking spray

7 tablespoons real egg substitute

⅔ cup fructose (fruit sugar, see p. 3), divided

7 tablespoons regular unsweetened cocoa

1½ teaspoons vanilla

5 egg whites

½ teaspoon cream of tartar

⅓ cup low-sugar red raspberry spread (or substitute any low-sugar, jam-type spread of your choice)

Confectioners' sugar

Adjust oven rack to center of oven and preheat oven to 325 degrees. Line a 10 by 15-inch jellyroll pan with cooking parchment and spray parchment and pan sides with non-stick cooking spray.

Combine egg substitute, ⅓ cup fructose, cocoa, and vanilla in bowl of electric mixer and beat until well mixed.

In separate bowl, beat egg whites until they hold soft peaks. Add cream of tartar and continue beating until they hold stiff peaks. With beaters running, add remaining ⅓ cup fructose in thin stream. As soon as sugar is added, turn off beaters.

Fold meringue into cocoa batter.

Spread batter in prepared pan and bake 20 to 25 minutes or until cake pulls away from side of pan.

Remove from oven and let stand 5 minutes in pan. Use a small knife to loosen cake from sides of pan if necessary. Turn out onto cooling rack. When cool, cut in half.

Spread raspberry jam on one half of cake and top with second half of cake. Cut cake into quarters; then cut each quarter into four pieces. Sprinkle with confectioners' sugar.

Nutritional Data

PER SERVING		EXCHANGES	
Calories:	47	Milk:	0.0
% Calories from fat:	6	Veg.:	0.0
Fat (gm):	0.3	Fruit:	0.5
Sat. fat (gm):	0	Bread:	0.0
Cholesterol (mg):	0	Meat:	0.5
Sodium (mg):	32	Fat:	0.0
Protein (gm):	3		
Carbohydrate (gm):	8		

CAKE ROLL WITH WHIPPED COCOA-BANANA FILLING

Chocolate tastes as good with bananas as it does with apples, oranges, and coffee flavors.

12 Servings

Non-stick cooking spray
1 cup cake flour, scant, sifted before measuring
1 tablespoon unsweetened Dutch cocoa
1 teaspoon baking powder
7 tablespoons real egg substitute
12 tablespoons (¾ cup) fructose (fruit sugar, see p. 3), divided
1 teaspoon vanilla extract
4 egg whites
½ teaspoon cream of tartar
Whipped Cocoa-Banana Filling (recipe follows)
2 medium bananas
Confectioners' sugar

Adjust oven rack to center of oven and preheat oven to 350 degrees. Line an 11½ x 17½-inch jellyroll pan with cooking parchment and spray parchment and sides of pan with non-stick cooking spray.

Sift flour again with cocoa and baking powder. Set aside.

Place real egg substitute, 6 tablespoons fructose, and vanilla in large bowl of electric mixer and beat until well mixed.

In separate bowl, beat egg whites until they hold soft peaks, add cream of tartar, and beat again until they hold stiff peaks. With beaters running, add remaining 6 tablespoons fructose in a thin stream. As soon as sugar is incorporated, turn beaters off.

Fold egg substitute mixture into meringue; then fold in flour mixture.

Spoon batter into prepared pan, and use spatula to smooth batter to edges and to smooth out holes in batter.

Bake 12 minutes or until edges are brown and cake tests done in center with bamboo skewer or cake tester.

Remove pan from oven and loosen cake sides with sharp knife. Invert cake onto kitchen towel that has been sprinkled with confectioners' sugar.

Fold towel over cake on all sides. Roll cake up in towel the long way. Allow to cool.

When cool, unroll and place on serving platter. Spread Whipped Cocoa-Banana Filling over cake roll. Slice bananas thinly and place slices on filling.

Re-roll carefully, cover, and refrigerate.

At serving time, sprinkle roll generously with confectioners' sugar and cut cake into quarters. Cut each quarter into three slices.

Whipped Cocoa-Banana Filling

Makes about 2½ cups

- 1 envelope dry whipped topping mix
- 4 teaspoons unsweetened Dutch cocoa
- ½ cup cold milk
  Chocolate extract, few drops
- ½ teaspoon vanilla extract

Place whipped topping mix and cocoa in large bowl of electric mixer and add cold milk. Use wire whisk to thoroughly combine.

Add chocolate and vanilla extracts and beat according to package directions until stiff.

Nutritional Data

PER SERVING		EXCHANGES	
Calories:	116	Milk:	0.0
% Calories from fat:	2	Veg.:	0.0
Fat (gm):	0.3	Fruit:	1.0
Sat. fat (gm):	0.1	Bread:	0.5
Cholesterol (mg):	0.2	Meat:	0.0
Sodium (mg):	68	Fat:	0.0
Protein (gm):	3		
Carbohydrate (gm):	24		

CHOCOLATE-FILLED CAKE ROLL

This cake roll is filled with a good-tasting chocolate sour cream mixture.

12 Servings

Non-stick cooking spray

6 large egg whites

¾ teaspoon cream of tartar

⅓ cup fructose (fruit sugar, see p. 3)

½ cup real egg substitute

1 teaspoon vanilla

6 tablespoons cake flour

Chocolate Sour Cream Filling (recipe follows)

Confectioners' sugar

Adjust oven rack to center of oven and preheat oven to 325 degrees. Line bottom of 17½ by 11½-inch jellyroll pan with parchment and spray pan sides and parchment with non-stick cooking spray.

In electric mixer bowl, beat egg whites until they hold soft peaks, add cream of tartar, and beat again until they hold stiff peaks. With beaters running, add fructose in thin stream. As soon as sugar is incorporated, turn beaters off.

In separate bowl, beat real egg substitute with vanilla until well mixed. Fold it into meringue. Then fold in cake flour.

Spread batter into prepared pan, and bake 15 minutes or until edges are light brown.

Use a sharp knife to loosen cake from edges of pan if necessary. Invert cake onto lightly dampened cotton towel.

Fold edges of towel over cake on all sides. Roll cake up in towel. Allow to cool.

When cool, place on serving platter and unroll, removing towel. Spread cake with Chocolate Sour Cream Filling and carefully re-roll.

Cover and refrigerate. At serving time, cut cake into quarters; cut each quarter into 3 slices. Sprinkle with confectioners' sugar.

Chocolate Sour Cream Filling

Makes about 2 cups

2 tablespoons unsweetened Dutch cocoa
1 tablespoon cornstarch
3 tablespoons skim milk
½ cup real egg substitute
¼ cup fructose (fruit sugar, see p. 3)
1¼ cups no-fat sour cream
1 teaspoon vanilla
2 teaspoons aspartame

Place cocoa and cornstarch with skim milk in top of double boiler. Use wire whisk to stir until well mixed. Stir in real egg substitute, fructose, and sour cream, mixing well.

Cook over simmering water, stirring with whisk, until thickened, about 5 minutes. Remove from heat and cool slightly before stirring in vanilla and aspartame.

Chill before using in Cake Roll (above).

Nutritional Data

PER SERVING		EXCHANGES	
Calories:	93	Milk:	0.0
% Calories from fat:	1	Veg.:	0.0
Fat (gm):	0.1	Fruit:	0.5
Sat. fat (gm):	trace	Bread:	0.5
Cholesterol (mg):	0.1	Meat:	0.5
Sodium (mg):	58	Fat:	0.0
Protein (gm):	6		
Carbohydrate (gm):	16		

DUTCH COCOA ROLL

This is a delicious and sophisticated cake roll, filled with ricotta and jam.

12 Servings

Non-stick cooking spray
7 tablespoons real egg substitute
⅔ cup fructose (fruit sugar, see p. 3), divided
7 tablespoons unsweetened Dutch cocoa
1 teaspoon vanilla extract
5 egg whites
½ teaspoon cream of tartar
Ricotta Cheese Filling (recipe follows)
Confectioners' sugar

Adjust oven rack to center of oven and preheat oven to 325 degrees. Line a 10 by 15-inch jellyroll pan with cooking parchment and spray parchment and pan sides with non-stick cooking spray.

Combine egg substitute, ⅓ cup fructose, cocoa, and vanilla in bowl of electric mixer and beat until well mixed.

In separate bowl, beat egg whites until they hold soft peaks. Add cream of tartar, and continue beating until they hold stiff peaks. With beaters running, add remaining ⅓ cup fructose in a thin stream. As soon as sugar has been added, turn off beaters.

Fold meringue into cocoa batter.

Spread batter in prepared pan and bake 20 to 25 minutes or until cake pulls away from sides of pan.

Remove from oven and let cool 5 minutes in pan. If necessary, use a sharp knife to loosen cake from sides of pan.

Turn out onto large, damp muslin towel. Carefully and slowly, peel off paper. Fold towel over the cake on all sides.

Roll cake (long side up) slowly in towel. Carefully place cake in refrigerator.

When cold, unroll cake carefully on serving platter.

Spread Ricotta Cheese Filling over cake and carefully re-roll. Cover with plastic wrap and refrigerate until chilled, about 2 hours.

At serving time, cut cake into quarters. Cut each quarter into 3 slices. Sprinkle slices with confectioners' sugar.

Ricotta Cheese Filling

1 container (15 ozs.) low-fat ricotta cheese
⅓ cup low-sugar strawberry jam (or any flavor desired)
1 tablespoon aspartame, or to taste

Place ricotta, jam, and aspartame in food processor and pulse until soft.

Nutritional Data

PER SERVING		EXCHANGES	
Calories:	94	Milk:	0.0
% Calories from fat:	12	Veg.:	0.0
Fat (gm):	1	Fruit:	1.0
Sat. fat (gm):	0.1	Bread:	0.0
Cholesterol (mg):	5	Meat:	0.5
Sodium (mg):	73	Fat:	0.0
Protein (gm):	7		
Carbohydrate (gm):	7		

COCOA GINGERBREAD CAKE

Richness is what cocoa adds to this classic gingerbread cake. A small amount of dried cherries or raisins can be added to the batter for elegance.

12 Servings

Non-stick, butter-flavored cooking spray
⅓ cup diet margarine
⅓ cup fructose (fruit sugar, see p. 3)
½ cup real egg substitute
½ cup molasses
1¾ cups all-purpose flour
⅓ cup cocoa
2 teaspoons baking powder
½ teaspoon baking soda
1¾ teaspoons grated fresh ginger
¾ teaspoon ground cinnamon
⅛ teaspoon ground nutmeg
¼ teaspoon salt
¾ cup buttermilk

Spray a 9 x 9-inch, non-stick baking pan. Preheat oven to 350 degrees.

Using an electric mixer, combine margarine and fructose. Blend in egg substitute, and molasses.

Sift flour, cocoa, baking powder, baking soda, ginger, cinnamon, nutmeg, and salt. Add dry ingredients to batter alternately with buttermilk. Batter should be smooth.

Pour batter into prepared pan. Bake in center of oven 35 to 45 minutes or until a tester inserted in cake comes out clean.

Cool cake 5 minutes in pan. Turn cake out by inverting onto wire rack; cool. Cut cake and serve. Good with a scoop of non-cholesterol vanilla ice cream.

Nutritional Data

PER SERVING		EXCHANGES	
Calories:	149	Milk:	0.0
% Calories from fat:	18	Veg.:	0.0
Fat (gm):	3	Fruit:	1.0
Sat. fat (gm):	0.6	Bread:	1.0
Cholesterol (mg):	0.6	Meat:	0.0
Sodium (mg):	229	Fat:	0.5
Protein (gm):	3		
Carbohydrate (gm):	28		

CHOCOLATE "SOUR CREAM" CAKE

Crème de cocoa is the flavoring for this cake. Naturally, we substituted non-fat sour cream for the original version.

8 Servings
Butter-flavored, non-stick cooking spray
1 teaspoon baking soda
¼ cup non-fat sour cream
3 tablespoons diet margarine
¼ cup unsweetened Dutch cocoa
½ cup fructose (fruit sugar, see p. 3)
¼ cup real egg substitute
2 teaspoons crème de cocoa liqueur
1 cup cake flour, sifted
½ cup hot water

Preheat oven to 350 degrees. Spray an 8-inch-square cake pan with butter-flavored, non-stick cooking spray.

In a mixing bowl, stir baking soda into sour cream; set aside.

Melt margarine with cocoa, stirring constantly over very low heat.

In separate bowl, whisk (or use electric mixer) together fructose and egg substitute until light and fluffy. Add crème de cocoa. Whisk in cocoa mixture. Add flour alternately with water, mixing thoroughly after each addition.

Pour mixture into prepared pan. Bake 25 to 30 minutes or until cake tests done with cake tester or small bamboo skewer. Cool on wire rack. Cut into squares and serve with sliced fresh fruit, if desired.

Nutritional Data

PER SERVING		EXCHANGES	
Calories:	130	Milk:	0.0
% Calories from fat:	21	Veg.:	0.0
Fat (gm):	3	Fruit:	0.5
Sat. fat (gm):	0.7	Bread:	1.0
Cholesterol (mg):	27	Meat:	0.0
Sodium (mg):	161	Fat:	0.5
Protein (gm):	3		
Carbohydrate (gm):	23		

FUDGE CAKE WITH COCOA ICING

What could be more appealing than a Fudge Cake with Cocoa Icing? It's baked in a 9- or 9½-inch springform pan. Or you can use two 9-inch layer cake pans and double the icing to frost cake.

10 Servings

Butter-flavored, non-stick cooking spray
- ½ cup cocoa
- ½ cup skim milk
- ⅓ cup diet margarine
- ½ cup fructose (fruit sugar, see p. 3)
- 1 teaspoon vanilla
- ¾ cup real egg substitute
- 2 cups cake flour, sifted
- 1½ teaspoons baking soda
- ¼ teaspoon salt
- ¾ cup buttermilk

Cocoa Icing (recipe follows)

Preheat oven to 350 degrees. Spray a 9-inch springform pan; line it tightly with aluminum foil and spray again.

In a small saucepan, whisk cocoa with milk. Scald milk over medium-low heat, whisking occasionally. Cool.

Using electric mixer bowl, beat margarine with fructose. Stir in cocoa mixture, vanilla, and egg substitute.

Sift flour, baking soda, and salt together. Add these dry ingredients alternately with buttermilk.

Pour batter into prepared pan. Bake in center of oven 40 minutes or until cake tests done when cake tester or bamboo skewer inserted in cake comes out dry.

Cool cake 5 minutes. Remove pan and cool cake completely on cake rack. Remove aluminum foil carefully.

Cocoa Icing

1 cup confectioners' sugar, sifted
3 tablespoons diet margarine
2 tablespoons unsweetened Dutch cocoa
¾ teaspoon vanilla
¼ teaspoon chocolate extract
2–3 tablespoons skim milk

While cake is cooling, prepare icing. Use food processor or electric mixer. If using food processor, it is not necessary to sift sugar. Place sugar, margarine, cocoa, vanilla, and chocolate extract in processor. Combine ingredients. Add milk until icing is desired thickness.

Spread icing over top of cake to edges, allowing it to drip down sides of cake. Slice and enjoy.

Nutritional Data

PER SERVING		EXCHANGES	
Calories:	222	Milk:	0.0
% Calories from fat:	22	Veg.:	0.0
Fat (gm):	6	Fruit:	0.5
Sat. fat (gm):	1	Bread:	2.0
Cholesterol (mg):	0.9	Meat:	0.0
Sodium (mg):	340	Fat:	1.0
Protein (gm):	6		
Carbohydrate (gm):	39		

CHOCOLATE CAKE WITH PUREED PRUNES

This is a moist, dense tea cake, thanks to the prunes, which supply a fruitcake-like flavor.

9 Servings

Butter-flavored, non-stick cooking spray
- ¼ cup diet margarine, room temperature
- ½ cup fructose (fruit sugar, see p. 3)
- ½ cup real egg substitute
- 1½ cups all-purpose flour
- 1½ cups unsweetened Dutch cocoa
- 1¼ teaspoons baking powder
- ¼ teaspoon each ingredient: baking soda and salt
- 1½ teaspoons fresh-squeezed lemon juice
- ½ cup skim milk
- 1 teaspoon vanilla
- 1¼ cups pitted, pureed prunes

P reheat oven to 375 degrees. Spray a 9-inch decorative ring mold. Cut margarine into small pieces; put in electric mixer bowl and blend in fructose and egg substitute.

Sift flour, cocoa, baking powder, baking soda, and salt. Set aside.

Stir lemon juice into milk. Add flour mixture to milk mixture. Add vanilla and pureed prunes.

Spoon batter into prepared pan. Bake in center of oven 40 minutes or until cake tests done. Cake is done when it springs back when lightly touched or tester comes out dry and clean.

Cool cake on wire rack.

Nutritional Data

PER SERVING		EXCHANGES	
Calories:	226	Milk:	0.0
% Calories from fat:	15	Veg.:	0.0
Fat (gm):	4	Fruit:	1.0
Sat. fat (gm):	0.8	Bread:	2.0
Cholesterol (mg):	0.2	Meat:	0.0
Sodium (mg):	225	Fat:	0.5
Protein (gm):	7		
Carbohydrate (gm):	47		

COCOA TEA CAKE

◆

Wrap cake before storing. Cut in slices, this cake is good with a dollop of chocolate light ice cream.

10 Servings

Butter-flavored, non-stick cooking spray
2 scant cups all-purpose flour
⅔ cups fructose (fruit sugar, see p. 3)
¼ cup unsweetened Dutch cocoa
1 teaspoon baking powder
1 teaspoon baking soda
¼ teaspoon salt
½ cup skim milk
½ cup plain non-fat yogurt
¼ cup real egg substitute
¼ cup canola blend (corn oil and canola oil packaged blend)
1 teaspoon vanilla
½ teaspoon chocolate extract
¼ cup raisins (optional)

Preheat oven to 350 degrees. Spray a 4½ x 8½ x 2½-inch pan. Set aside.

In large bowl of electric mixer, combine flour, fructose, cocoa, baking powder, baking soda, and salt. Blend in milk, yogurt, egg substitute, oil, vanilla, chocolate extract, and raisins (optional).

Pour batter into prepared pan. Bake in center of oven 55 to 60 minutes or until done. Cake will spring back when lightly touched or test dry with cake tester or bamboo skewer.

Cool cake on rack. Slice thin and serve with sliced fruit or a dollop of chocolate light ice cream.

Nutritional Data

PER SERVING		EXCHANGES	
Calories:	198	Milk:	0.0
% Calories from fat:	27	Veg.:	0.0
Fat (gm):	6	Fruit:	0.5
Sat. fat (gm):	0.7	Bread:	1.5
Cholesterol (mg):	0.4	Meat:	0.0
Sodium (mg):	111	Fat:	1.0
Protein (gm):	5		
Carbohydrate (gm):	32		

CHOCOLATE TEA CAKE WITH ITALIAN MERINGUE FROSTING

This cake is good looking as well as good to eat. We used an 8-inch cake pan with removable side and a tube center. Try making an "English Tea Party"; serve watercress and cucumber sandwiches with Chocolate Tea Cake for dessert.

10 Servings

Butter-flavored, non-stick cooking spray
¾ cup fructose (fruit sugar, see p. 3)
3 tablespoons diet margarine, cut into cubes, room temperature
1 tablespoon canola oil
¼ cup real egg substitute
1 egg white
1¾ cups sifted cake flour
¼ cup unsweetened Dutch cocoa
1 teaspoon baking powder
¼ teaspoon salt
¾ teaspoon vanilla
½ teaspoon chocolate extract
½ cup non-fat vanilla yogurt
Italian Meringue Frosting (recipe follows)

Preheat oven to 350 degrees. Coat with cooking spray an 8-inch cake pan with removable side and tube center. Set aside.

Using an electric mixer, blend fructose, margarine, and oil. Add egg substitute and egg white.

Sift flour with cocoa, baking powder, and salt onto paper plate or into bowl. Blend dry ingredients into batter. Add vanilla, chocolate extract, and yogurt.

Spoon batter into prepared pan. Bake cake in center of oven 30 to 35 minutes or until cake tests done (a small bamboo skewer or cake tester will come out clean).

Cool cake on wire rack. Remove pan and carefully invert cake onto serving dish. Brush off any crumbs and frost.

Italian Meringue Frosting

½ cup sugar

1 tablespoon light corn syrup

2 tablespoons water

2 egg whites, room temperature

¼ teaspoon cream of tartar

¼ teaspoon vanilla

½ teaspoon chocolate extract

While cake is cooling, prepare frosting.

Blend sugar, corn syrup, and water together in small, heavy saucepan. Cover tightly and cook over medium heat 2 minutes. Uncover and continue cooking until a candy thermometer registers 240 degrees, or mixture reaches soft-ball stage.

Meanwhile, in large bowl of electric mixer, beat egg whites until soft peaks form. Sprinkle whites with cream of tartar and beat until firm peaks form. With whites beating on high, drizzle boiling sugar solution into whites. Mix in vanilla and chocolate extract. Continue beating a few minutes only, until frosting is cool and stiff peaks form.

Mound frosting over cake.

Nutritional Data

PER SERVING		EXCHANGES	
Calories:	208	Milk:	0.0
% Calories from fat:	15	Veg.:	0.0
Fat (gm):	3	Fruit:	0.5
Sat. fat (gm):	0.5	Bread:	2.0
Cholesterol (mg):	0.3	Meat:	0.0
Sodium (mg):	160	Fat:	0.5
Protein (gm):	4		
Carbohydrate (gm):	41		

MARBLE CAKE

All recipes are tested with fresh egg whites, which produce a greater volume than egg substitute when beaten. Marble cake incorporates ribbons of chocolate and vanilla swished together in a loaf shape.

10 Servings

Butter-flavored, non-stick cooking spray
⅓ cup diet margarine, room temperature
¾ cup fructose (fruit sugar, see p. 3)
1 teaspoon vanilla
1¾ cups cake flour, sifted
2 teaspoons baking soda
¼ teaspoon salt
¾ cup skim milk
3 egg whites, beaten stiff
¼ cup unsweetened Dutch cocoa
2 tablespoons hot water
¼ teaspoon baking soda
1 tablespoon fructose

Preheat oven to 350 degrees. Spray a loaf pan.

Using electric mixer, beat margarine, fructose, and vanilla.

Sift flour again with baking soda and salt. We use a strainer and sift onto a sheet of waxed paper or paper plate.

Add flour mixture alternately with milk to margarine/vanilla mixture. Fold in beaten egg whites.

In small bowl, blend cocoa, water, baking soda, and fructose.

Divide batter in half. Stir cocoa mixture into one-half of batter.

Pour other half of batter into pan. Drop cocoa batter by tablespoons in dollops over vanilla batter. With a knife, swirl cocoa batter through vanilla batter.

Bake in center of oven 55 to 60 minutes. Cake is done when a tester or bamboo skewer inserted in center comes out dry. Cool cake on wire rack. Slice and serve. Always good with sliced fruit.

Nutritional Data

PER SERVING		EXCHANGES	
Calories:	160	Milk:	0.0
% Calories from fat:	19	Veg.:	0.0
Fat (gm):	3	Fruit:	1.0
Sat. fat (gm):	0.6	Bread:	1.0
Cholesterol (mg):	0.3	Meat:	0.0
Sodium (mg):	335	Fat:	0.5
Protein (gm):	4		
Carbohydrate (gm):	29		

PEACH UPSIDE-DOWN CAKE

To remove cake from pan, run a knife around the pan edges. Place serving plate on top of cake pan, and, with a quick wrist movement, invert cake onto plate. If any sauce drips onto plate, spoon it over cake as you serve it. This cake is also good made with canned pineapple or cherries.

9 Servings

Butter-flavored, non-stick cooking spray
3 tablespoons diet margarine, melted
¼ cup, firmly packed, dark brown sugar
2 cups peeled peaches, sliced
½ cup real egg substitute
¼ cup sugar
2 tablespoons fructose (fruit sugar, see p. 3)
1¼ cups all-purpose flour
¼ cup unsweetened cocoa
¾ teaspoon baking soda
½ teaspoon baking powder
¼ teaspoon salt
½ cup skim milk
1 teaspoon vanilla
¼ teaspoon chocolate extract

P reheat oven to 350 degrees. Spray a 9-inch layer cake pan. Drizzle melted margarine over bottom of pan; sprinkle with brown sugar.

To peel peaches, dip in boiling water or run under hot water for a few seconds. Skins should slip off under slight pressure.

In large bowl of electric mixer, combine egg substitute, sugar, and fructose. Blend in flour, cocoa, baking soda, baking powder, and salt. Add milk, vanilla, and chocolate extract.

Place sliced peaches in bottom of cake pan, and pour batter over peaches. Bake cake in center of oven 35 minutes. Cake is done when cake tester or bamboo skewer inserted in cake comes out clean.

Let cake cool 5 minutes. To remove cake, see instructions at top of recipe. Serve warm or at room temperature.

Nutritional Data

PER SERVING

		EXCHANGES	
Calories:	164	Milk:	0.0
% Calories from fat:	12	Veg.:	0.0
Fat (gm):	2	Fruit:	0.5
Sat. fat (gm):	0.4	Bread:	1.5
Cholesterol (mg):	0.2	Meat:	0.0
Sodium (mg):	218	Fat:	0.5
Protein (gm):	4		
Carbohydrate (gm):	33		

2.
ANGEL CAKES

Chocolate Angel Food Cake
♦
Mocha Angel Cake
♦
Half Angel Cake
♦
Angel Cassata à la Siciliana
♦
Angel Cupcakes
♦
Chocolate Jellyroll with Homemade Raspberry Jam
♦
Baked Chocolate Alaska
♦
Spicy Angel Cake Torte

CHOCOLATE ANGEL FOOD CAKE

Although we use sugar (for volume), there is no fat in this recipe. Let egg whites stand at room temperature 30 minutes before using.

12 Servings

- 1½ cups egg whites, room temperature
- 1 teaspoon cream of tartar
- 1 cup sugar, divided
- ¼ teaspoon salt
- 1 teaspoon vanilla
- ½ teaspoon chocolate extract
- ¾ cup cake flour, sifted
- ¼ cup unsweetened Dutch cocoa

Preheat oven to 350 degrees. Cut sheet of waxed paper to fit bottom of 10-inch tube cake pan.

Beat egg whites in large bowl of electric mixer until light. Blend in cream of tartar and 3 tablespoons sugar. Continue beating and adding sugar until all but 1 tablespoon of sugar has been incorporated and egg whites are firm. Mix in salt, vanilla, and chocolate extract.

Onto sheet of waxed paper or paper plate, sift flour again with remaining sugar and cocoa.

Sprinkle flour mixture, in thirds, over egg whites. Using rubber spatula, with deep strokes and twisting spatula as you stir, incorporate flour mixture into egg whites. Do not over mix, as you do not want to deflate egg whites. Spoon batter into prepared pan.

Bake cake in center of oven 50 to 55 minutes or until cake is lightly browned on top and springs back when gently touched; or use cake tester.

Cake must cool inverted; tube pan has "legs" to provide for this. Remove cake from pan when cooled completely. Cut with serrated knife.

Angel cake does not freeze well. Wrapped tightly, it will store 3 or 4 days.

Nutritional Data

PER SERVING		EXCHANGES	
Calories:	104	Milk:	0.0
% Calories from fat:	2	Veg.:	0.0
Fat (gm):	0.2	Fruit:	0.0
Sat. fat (gm):	0.1	Bread:	1.5
Cholesterol (mg):	0	Meat:	0.0
Sodium (mg):	92	Fat:	0.0
Protein (gm):	4		
Carbohydrate (gm):	23		

MOCHA ANGEL CAKE

Angel cake is special because it is prepared without any oil or butter. Egg whites give this cake its height.

12 Servings

- 1½ cups egg whites, room temperature, about 10 to 12 egg whites
- 1 teaspoon cream of tartar
- 1 cup sugar, divided
- ¼ teaspoon salt
- 1¼ teaspoon vanilla
- ¾ cup cake flour, sifted
- ¼ cup Dutch processed cocoa
- 2 teaspoons instant coffee
- ½ teaspoon ground cinnamon

Preheat oven to 350 degrees. Cut sheet of waxed paper to fit bottom of 10-inch tube cake pan.

Beat egg whites in large bowl of electric mixer until light. Blend in cream of tartar and 3 tablespoons sugar. Continue beating and adding sugar until all but 1 tablespoon of sugar has been incorporated and egg whites are firm. Mix in salt and vanilla.

Onto sheet of waxed paper or paper plate, sift flour again with remaining sugar and cocoa, coffee, and cinnamon.

Sprinkle flour mixture, in thirds, over egg whites. Using rubber spatula, with deep strokes and twisting spatula as you stir, incorporate flour mixture into egg whites. Do not over mix, as you do not want to deflate egg whites. Spoon batter into prepared pan.

Bake cake in center of oven 50 to 55 minutes or until cake is lightly browned on top and springs back when gently touched; or use cake tester.

Cake must cool inverted; tube pan has "legs" to provide for this. Remove cake from pan when cooled completely. Cut with serrated knife.

Angel cake does not freeze well. Wrapped tightly, it will store 3 or 4 days.

Nutritional Data

PER SERVING		EXCHANGES	
Calories:	105	Milk:	0.0
% Calories from fat:	2	Veg.:	0.0
Fat (gm):	0.2	Fruit:	0.0
Sat. fat (gm):	0.1	Bread:	1.5
Cholesterol (mg):	0	Meat:	0.0
Sodium (mg):	92	Fat:	0.0
Protein (gm):	4		
Carbohydrate (gm):	23		

HALF ANGEL CAKE

This cocoa tube cake has the delicacy of an angel food without the egg whites.

12 Servings

1½ cups cake flour, sifted before measuring
3 tablespoons unsweetened Dutch cocoa
1½ teaspoons baking powder
¾ cup plus 6 tablespoons fructose (fruit sugar, see p. 3), divided
¾ cup plus 2 tablespoons skim milk
¼ teaspoon, scant, almond extract
¾ teaspoon vanilla extract
4 egg whites
½ teaspoon cream of tartar
Confectioners' sugar

Adjust oven rack to center of oven and preheat oven to 350 degrees. Sift flour, cocoa, baking powder, and ¾ cup fructose into large bowl of electric mixer.

In separate bowl, combine milk and almond and vanilla extracts. Add to dry ingredients in two batches, beating after each addition.

Beat egg whites until they hold soft peaks; add cream of tartar and beat again until they hold stiff peaks. With beaters running, add remaining 6 tablespoons fructose in thin stream. As soon as sugar is incorporated, turn beaters off.

Fold meringue into batter. Spoon into 10-inch ungreased tube cake pan with removable bottom, and bake at 350 degrees about 30 minutes or until top of cake springs back when pressed lightly with fingertip.

Remove from oven and invert pan for 1 hour to cool. Use sharp knife to loosen cake from sides of pan. Remove cake and allow it to finish cooling right side up on wire rack.

When cool, cut cake into quarters. Cut each quarter into three pieces. Sprinkle cake with confectioners' sugar before serving.

Nutritional Data

PER SERVING		EXCHANGES	
Calories:	120	Milk:	0.0
% Calories from fat:	2	Veg.:	0.0
Fat (gm):	0.3	Fruit:	1.0
Sat. fat (gm):	0.1	Bread:	1.0
Cholesterol (mg):	0.3	Meat:	0.0
Sodium (mg):	70	Fat:	0.0
Protein (gm):	3		
Carbohydrate (gm):	26		

Angel Cassata à la Siciliana

A classic cassata is horizontally sliced pound cake filled with sweetened ricotta cheese and then frosted. We used an angel cake prepared in a loaf pan, lightened the filling, and omitted the frosting.

8 Servings

¾ cup (about 5 or 6) egg whites, room temperature
½ teaspoon cream of tartar
8 tablespoons sugar
¼ teaspoon salt
¾ teaspoon vanilla
½ cup cake flour, sifted
2½ tablespoons unsweetened Dutch cocoa
½ teaspoon ground cinnamon
Filling (recipe follows)

P reheat oven to 350 degrees. Cut piece of waxed paper to fit bottom of 9 x 5 x 3-inch-deep loaf pan. This is not necessary if loaf pan is non-stick and spray coated.

Beat egg whites in large bowl of electric mixer until light. Sprinkle cream of tartar and 3 tablespoons sugar over egg whites and incorporate. Continue beating, while adding 2 tablespoons sugar, until egg whites are firm. Mix in salt and vanilla.

Sift flour again with remaining sugar, cocoa, and cinnamon onto sheet of waxed paper or paper plate.

Sprinkle flour mixture, in thirds, over egg whites. Using rubber spatula, make deep stirring strokes, twisting spatula as you mix flour mixture into egg whites. Do not over mix, as you do not want to deflate egg whites.

Pour batter into loaf pan. Bake cake in center of oven about 30 minutes or until cake is brown on top and springs back when gently touched; or use cake tester.

Cake must cool inverted, so arrange 4 short glasses or coffee cups to support corners of loaf pan. Remove cake from pan when it has cooled completely. Cut cake horizontally with serrated knife to make 3 layers.

Filling
3 tablespoons golden raisins
2 tablespoons dark rum or sherry
10 ozs. non-fat ricotta cheese
2 tablespoons fructose (fruit sugar, see p. 3)
1 teaspoon orange rind, grated
1 teaspoon confectioners' sugar, sifted (optional)

Prepare filling while cake is cooling.

Soak raisins in rum. Put cheese in bowl and add drained raisins, fructose, and orange rind. Mix well.

Spread half of filling over bottom layer of cake. Gently arrange second layer of cake on top. Again gently spread with filling. Set top layer of cake in place. Sprinkle with confectioners' sugar if desired. Slice with serrated knife.

Nutritional Data

PER SERVING		EXCHANGES	
Calories:	166	Milk:	0.0
% Calories from fat:	16	Veg.:	0.0
Fat (gm):	3	Fruit:	0.0
Sat. fat (gm):	2	Bread:	2.0
Cholesterol (mg):	11	Meat:	0.5
Sodium (mg):	147	Fat:	0.0
Protein (gm):	7		
Carbohydrate (gm):	27		

ANGEL CUPCAKES

The cupcake is just what the name implies, a light, delicate morsel of cake. You can sprinkle with confectioners' sugar or top with 1 teaspoon of chocolate sauce just before serving.

18 Servings, 1 cupcake each

- ¾ cup egg whites, about 5–6, room temperature
- ½ teaspoon cream of tartar
- ½ cup sugar, divided
- ¼ teaspoon salt
- ¾ teaspoon vanilla
- ½ cup, scant, cake flour, sifted
- 2½ tablespoons unsweetened Dutch cocoa
- ¼ teaspoon ground nutmeg
- ⅛ teaspoon ground allspice

Preheat oven to 350 degrees. Do not use cupcake liners because cupcakes must cool inverted and will fall out of pan if in liners.

Beat egg whites in large bowl of electric mixer until light. Sprinkle cream of tartar and 3 tablespoons sugar over egg whites; beat to incorporate. Continue adding sugar until all has been incorporated and egg whites are firm. Mix in salt and vanilla.

Onto sheet of waxed paper or paper plate, sift flour again with cocoa, nutmeg, and allspice.

Using rubber spatula, sprinkle flour mixture, in thirds, over egg whites. Using deep, twisting motion with spatula, incorporate flour mixture lightly into egg whites. Do not over mix, as you do not want to deflate egg whites.

Bake cupcakes in center of oven 15 to 20 minutes or until cakes spring back when gently touched; or use cake tester.

Cupcakes must cool inverted. Arrange 4 cups or glasses to support corners of inverted pan. Remove cakes from pan when cooled completely.

Nutritional Data

PER SERVING		EXCHANGES	
Calories:	38	Milk:	0.0
% Calories from fat:	3	Veg.:	0.0
Fat (gm):	0.1	Fruit:	0.0
Sat. fat (gm):	trace	Bread:	0.5
Cholesterol (mg):	0	Meat:	0.0
Sodium (mg):	45	Fat:	0.0
Protein (gm):	1		
Carbohydrate (gm):	8		

CHOCOLATE JELLYROLL WITH HOMEMADE RASPBERRY JAM

We use our angel cake for the jellyroll, baking it in a lined cookie sheet. Roll it up while cake is still warm so that it will cool in a rolled shape.

12 Servings

- 1½ cups egg whites, about 10–12, room temperature
- 1 teaspoon cream of tartar
- 1 cup, scant, sugar, divided
- ¼ teaspoon salt
- ¾ teaspoon vanilla
- ¾ cup cake flour, sifted
- ½ teaspoon chocolate extract
- ¼ cup unsweetened Dutch cocoa
- **Raspberry Jam** (recipe follows), or light fruit spread (8 calories per serving)

 Preheat oven to 350 degrees. Cut sheet of waxed paper to fit bottom of standard cookie sheet.

Beat egg whites in large bowl of electric mixer until light. Sprinkle cream of tartar and 3 tablespoons sugar over egg whites; beat to incorporate. Continue adding 9 more tablespoons sugar while beating, until egg whites are firm. Mix in salt and vanilla.

Onto sheet of waxed paper or paper plate, sift flour again with remaining sugar, chocolate extract, and cocoa.

Using rubber spatula, sprinkle flour mixture, in thirds, over egg whites. Using deep, twisting motion with spatula, incorporate flour mixture lightly into egg whites. Do not over mix, as you do not want to deflate egg whites. Spoon batter into prepared cookie sheet.

Bake cake in center of oven 30 minutes or until cake springs back when touched gently; or use cake tester.

Spread clean towel on counter. Transfer cake onto towel. Spread jam evenly over entire cake. Roll cake, using towel as guide. Carefully transfer cake to serving dish. Cool. Sprinkle with confectioners' sugar, if desired. Slice and serve.

Raspberry Jam

Makes 2 half-pints

 1 pkg. (1½ teaspoons) unflavored gelatin
1½ tablespoons cold water
 3 cups raspberries washed, drained (or berries of
    your choice)
 ½ cup fructose
 1 tablespoon lemon juice, fresh-squeezed
 1 teaspoon lemon rind, grated
 2 half-pint jars, sterilized; keep hot
 2 teaspoons aspartame

Stir gelatin into cold water. Let stand 5 minutes.

Combine raspberries and fructose in sauce pan, and cook over medium-high heat until mixture boils. Remove pan from heat. Stir in gelatin and cook about 1 minute more. Stir in lemon juice and rind.

Immediately spoon jelly into prepared jars. Cover. Cool and refrigerate. Use in 1 week to 10 days; do not freeze.

To sweeten, add up to 2 teaspoons aspartame, to taste, after jam has cooled.

◆

Nutritional Data

PER SERVING		EXCHANGES	
Calories:	107	Milk:	0.0
% Calories from fat:	2	Veg.:	0.0
Fat (gm):	0.2	Fruit:	0.0
Sat. fat (gm):	0.1	Bread:	1.5
Cholesterol (mg):	0	Meat:	0.0
Sodium (mg):	100	Fat:	0.0
Protein (gm):	4		
Carbohydrate (gm):	23		

BAKED CHOCOLATE ALASKA

Keep this cake frozen until you are ready to top it with meringue and bake. Work quickly so the ice cream does not soften. Sugar is used in this recipe because volume is necessary.

10 Servings

¾ cup egg whites, about 5–6, room temperature
½ cup sugar
¼ teaspoon salt
½ teaspoon vanilla
½ teaspoon chocolate extract
¾ cups cake flour, sifted
3 tablespoons unsweetened Dutch cocoa
1 qt. non-cholesterol chocolate ice cream
Meringue (recipe follows)

Preheat oven to 350 degrees. Cut sheet of waxed paper to fit bottom of loaf pan. This is not necessary if pan is spray coated.

Beat egg whites in large bowl of electric mixer until light. Sprinkle cream of tartar and 3 tablespoons sugar over egg whites; beat to incorporate. Continue adding sugar until all has been incorporated and egg whites are firm. Mix in salt, vanilla, and chocolate extract.

Onto sheet of waxed paper or paper plate, sift flour again with cocoa.

Sprinkle flour mixture, in thirds, over egg whites. Using rubber spatula and deep, twisting motion, incorporate flour mixture into egg whites. Do not over mix as you do not want to deflate egg whites. Spoon batter into prepared pan.

Bake cake in center of oven about 30 minutes or until cake springs back when gently touched; or use cake tester.

Cake must cool inverted. Arrange 4 cups to support inverted pan. Remove cake from pan when cool.

Using serrated knife, slice cake in half. Serve one-half at another meal.

Place remaining half of cake on non-stick cookie sheet. Top with ice cream, leaving ½-inch border. Freeze cake and ice cream.

Meringue
5 egg whites
½ teaspoon cream of tartar
¼ cup fructose (fruit sugar, see p. 3)
1 teaspoon vanilla

When ready to serve Baked Alaska, preheat oven to 450 degrees.

Beat egg whites until soft peaks form. Sprinkle cream of tartar and fructose over whites. Continue beating until fructose is absorbed. Sprinkle vanilla over whites and continue beating until firm peaks form.

Working quickly, take cake from freezer and cover with meringue, sealing edges completely. Place cake in oven and bake 4 minutes or until meringue is golden brown. Slide Baked Alaska onto serving plate, slice, and serve immediately.

Nutritional Data

PER SERVING		EXCHANGES	
Calories:	186	Milk:	0.0
% Calories from fat:	5	Veg.:	0.0
Fat (gm):	1	Fruit:	0.0
Sat. fat (gm):	trace	Bread:	2.5
Cholesterol (mg):	0	Meat:	0.0
Sodium (mg):	110	Fat:	0.0
Protein (gm):	7		
Carbohydrate (gm):	37		

SPICY ANGEL CAKE TORTE

Bake an angel cake in a loaf pan; slice it into 3 layers; fill it with prepared chocolate filling; reassemble and serve. To store cake, wrap in plastic wrap, and then in plastic storage container. It will keep 3 or 4 days.

---

8 Servings

¾ cup egg whites, about 5–6, room temperature
½ teaspoon cream of tartar
½ cup sugar
¼ teaspoon salt
½ teaspoon vanilla
¾ cup cake flour, sifted
3 tablespoons unsweetened Dutch cocoa
½ teaspoon ground cinnamon
¼ teaspoon each ingredient: ground nutmeg, cloves, allspice
Filling (recipe follows)

P reheat oven to 350 degrees. Cut sheet of waxed paper to fit bottom of loaf pan. This is not necessary if pan is spray coated.

Beat egg whites in large bowl of electric mixer until light. Sprinkle cream of tartar and 3 tablespoons sugar over egg whites; beat to incorporate. Continue adding sugar until all has been incorporated and egg whites are firm. Mix in salt and vanilla.

Onto sheet of waxed paper or paper plate, sift flour again with cocoa and spices.

Sprinkle flour mixture, in thirds, over egg whites. Using rubber spatula and deep, twisting motion, incorporate flour mixture into egg whites. Do not over mix, as you do not want to deflate egg whites. Spoon batter into prepared pan.

Bake cake in center of oven about 30 minutes or until cake springs back when gently touched; or use cake tester.

Cake must cool inverted. Arrange 4 cups to support inverted pan. Remove cake from pan when cooled completely. Cut cake horizontally into 3 layers.

Filling

1 pkg. sugar-free Jello Chocolate Pudding and Pie Filling
2 cups skim milk

While cake is cooling, prepare filling according to Jello package directions, using skim milk. Cool.

To prepare Torte, spread first layer of cake with one-third of pudding. Gentle repeat until Torte is complete. Cut with serrated knife.

Nutritional Data

PER SERVING		EXCHANGES	
Calories:	130	Milk:	0.0
% Calories from fat:	3	Veg.:	0.0
Fat (gm):	0.4	Fruit:	0.0
Sat. fat (gm):	0.2	Bread:	1.5
Cholesterol (mg):	1	Meat:	0.5
Sodium (mg):	186	Fat:	0.0
Protein (gm):	6		
Carbohydrate (gm):	27		

3.
CHOCOLATE PIES

Chocolate Sour Cream Pie
♦
Chocolate Yogurt Cherry Pie
♦
Chocolate Yogurt Pineapple Pie
♦
Mocha Chiffon Pie
♦
Plum and Cherry Clafouti
♦
Tofu Cocoa Pie
♦
Southern Mud Pie
♦
Cocoa Plum Crisp

61

CHOCOLATE SOUR CREAM PIE

The no-fat sour creams on the market are so excellent that no one will be able to tell the difference between the traditional and no-fat varieties, especially in this pie.

8 Servings

Crust
- 2 tablespoons diet margarine
- ½ cup graham cracker crumbs

Filling
- 2 tablespoons unsweetened Dutch cocoa
- 1½ teaspoons cornstarch
- ¾ teaspoon cinnamon
- Allspice, large pinch
- Nutmeg, large pinch
- 3 tablespoons skim milk
- ⅓ cup real egg substitute
- ¼ cup fructose (fruit sugar, see p. 3)
- 1 cup no-fat sour cream
- ¼ teaspoon vanilla

Meringue
- 2 large egg whites
- ¼ teaspoon cream of tartar
- ¼ cup confectioners' sugar

Adjust oven rack to center of oven and preheat oven to 350 degrees.

Crust: Melt margarine and add graham cracker crumbs, mixing well. Pat onto bottom of 9-inch pie plate. Bake 5 minutes. Remove pan, and lower heat to 300 degrees.

Filling: Combine cocoa, cornstarch, cinnamon, allspice, and nutmeg with skim milk, stirring with wire whisk until smooth.

Place egg substitute and fructose in top of double boiler and mix well with wire whisk. Add cocoa mixture and mix again until well combined. Stir in sour cream and vanilla.

Cook over simmering water, stirring constantly, until thickened. Spoon into prepared pie shell.

Return pie to oven at 300 degrees and bake 15 minutes. Remove from oven and cool to just warm. Continue to heat oven to 300 degrees.

Meringue: Beat egg whites until they hold soft peaks. Add cream of tartar and beat until they hold stiff peaks. With beaters running, add confectioners' sugar by spoonfuls. As soon as sugar is incorporated, turn beaters off.

Use a spatula to swirl meringue attractively over top of pie. Return to oven and bake 15 minutes or until delicately browned on top.

Remove from oven. Serve immediately or chill.

At serving time, cut pie into quarters. Cut each quarter into 2 pieces.

Nutritional Data

PER SERVING		EXCHANGES	
Calories:	106	Milk:	0.0
% Calories from fat:	20	Veg.:	0.0
Fat (gm):	2	Fruit:	0.0
Sat. fat (gm):	0.3	Bread:	1.0
Cholesterol (mg):	0.1	Meat:	0.5
Sodium (mg):	119	Fat:	0.0
Protein (gm):	6		
Carbohydrate (gm):	16		

CHOCOLATE YOGURT CHERRY PIE

This good-tasting pie has a strong chocolate flavor. If you prefer a fainter taste, reduce cocoa to 3 tablespoons.

12 Servings

Crust
3 tablespoons diet margarine
⅔ cup graham cracker crumbs

Filling
¼ cup unsweetened Dutch cocoa
⅓ cup water
1 cup non-fat, vanilla flavored aspartame-sweetened yogurt, at room temperature
1 teaspoon aspartame sweetener
½ teaspoon vanilla extract
1 can (15–16 ozs.) dark, sweet cherries
1 envelope plus 1½ teaspoons unflavored gelatin
1 envelope whipped topping mix
½ cup skim milk, cold

Arrange oven rack in center of oven and preheat oven to 350 degrees.

Crust: Melt margarine and add graham cracker crumbs, mixing well. Pat crumbs onto bottom of 10-inch pie pan. Bake 5 minutes. Remove from oven.

Filling: Place cocoa in bowl with water and stir with whisk until smooth. Add yogurt, mixing well. Stir in aspartame and vanilla.

Drain cherries, reserving juice.

Place gelatin in small bowl. Add ¼ cup cherry juice to soften. Heat remaining cherry juice to boil and stir into gelatin, mixing well until thoroughly incorporated.

Combine gelatin with cocoa/yogurt mixture and refrigerate, covered, until mixture has thickened.

Cut cherries into quarters.

Place whipped topping in bowl of electric mixer. Sprinkle with skim milk and stir with whisk until thoroughly mixed. Beat according to package directions until topping is thick.

Beat gelatin/cocoa/yogurt mixture with wire whisk until fluffy. Add to whipped topping and mix on slow speed until combined. Stir cherries into mixture.

Spoon into prepared crust, cover, and refrigerate at least 4 hours or until set. Cut pie into quarters, then cut each quarter into three pieces.

Nutritional Data

PER SERVING		EXCHANGES	
Calories:	87	Milk:	0.5
% Calories from fat:	21	Veg.:	0.0
Fat (gm):	2	Fruit:	0.5
Sat. fat (gm):	0.4	Bread:	0.0
Cholesterol (mg):	0.7	Meat:	0.0
Sodium (mg):	80	Fat:	0.0
Protein (gm):	3		
Carbohydrate (gm):	14		

CHOCOLATE YOGURT PINEAPPLE PIE

The pineapple adds a bright, acidic note to the chocolate flavor in this pie.

12 Servings

Crust

3 tablespoons diet margarine
⅔ cup graham cracker crumbs

Filling

1 can (20 ozs.) crushed pineapple, packed in unsweetened pineapple juice
¼ cup unsweetened Dutch cocoa
2½ cups non-fat yogurt, at room temperature
1 teaspoon aspartame sweetener
1 envelope plus 1½ teaspoons unflavored gelatin
½ cup graham cracker crumbs

Adjust oven rack to center of oven and preheat oven to 350 degrees.
Crust: Melt margarine and combine with graham cracker crumbs. Pat crumbs onto bottom of 10-inch pie plate, reserving 2 tablespoons. Bake 5 minutes. Remove from oven and allow to cool.

Filling: Drain pineapple and reserve juice. Press with spatula or wooden spoon to extract additional juice. Set pineapple aside.

Place cocoa in small bowl along with ¼ cup pineapple juice. Stir with whisk until smooth.

In separate bowl, beat yogurt with whisk until no lumps remain. Add cocoa mixture and aspartame sweetener.

Place gelatin in small bowl and sprinkle with ¼ cup pineapple juice to soften. Bring remaining pineapple juice to boil and pour over gelatin. Stir until completely dissolved.

Stir gelatin into cocoa/yogurt mixture, mixing well. Refrigerate until consistency of thick egg whites.

Remove from refrigerator and combine with crushed pineapple.

Spoon filling into prepared crust, and sprinkle remaining crumbs over top. Cover and refrigerate at least 4 hours or until set.

At serving time, cut pie into quarters, then cut each quarter into three pieces.

Nutritional Data

PER SERVING		EXCHANGES	
Calories:	113	Milk:	0.5
% Calories from fat:	19	Veg.:	0.0
Fat (gm):	2	Fruit:	1.0
Sat. fat (gm):	0.5	Bread:	0.0
Cholesterol (mg):	0.8	Meat:	0.0
Sodium (mg):	117	Fat:	0.5
Protein (gm):	5		
Carbohydrate (gm):	19		

MOCHA CHIFFON PIE

This pie is made with fructose sugar. But if you wish to substitute aspartame, eliminate fructose and stir 3½ teaspoons of aspartame into the coffee/cocoa mixture just before you fold in the whipped topping.

8 Servings

Crust

3 tablespoons diet margarine
⅔ cup graham cracker crumbs

Filling

2 tablespoons unsweetened Dutch cocoa
1 cup strong black coffee, warm
½ cup fructose (fruit sugar, see p. 3)
6 tablespoons real egg substitute
¼ cup water
1 envelope plus ¼ teaspoon unflavored gelatin
1 envelope whipped topping
½ cup skim milk, cold

Adjust oven rack to center of oven and preheat oven to 350 degrees.
Crust: Melt margarine and add crumbs. Stir until well combined. Pat crumbs onto bottom of 9-inch pie plate. Place in oven and bake 5 minutes. Remove from oven and allow to cool.

Filling: Place cocoa in heavy-bottomed pan and add 2 tablespoons coffee. Stir until smooth; then add remaining coffee and fructose. Stir in egg substitute. Cook over low heat, stirring constantly, until mixture thickens enough to lightly coat a spoon.

Place ¼ cup water in top of double boiler, and sprinkle gelatin over water to soften. Melt gelatin over simmering water.

When completely melted, stir gelatin into cocoa/coffee mixture. Allow to cool.

Place whipped topping in electric mixer bowl. Add skim milk and stir well with wire whisk to combine. Beat according to package directions until topping is thick.

If using aspartame, stir it into cocoa/coffee mixture at this point. Then fold whipped topping into mixture.

Spoon filling into baked pie shell. Refrigerate 4 hours or until firm. Cut pie into quarters; cut each quarter in half.

Nutritional Data

PER SERVING		EXCHANGES	
Calories:	122	Milk:	0.0
% Calories from fat:	22	Veg.:	0.0
Fat (gm):	3	Fruit:	0.5
Sat. fat (gm):	0.5	Bread:	1.0
Cholesterol (mg):	0.3	Meat:	0.0
Sodium (mg):	120	Fat:	0.5
Protein (gm):	3		
Carbohydrate (gm):	20		

Plum and Cherry Clafouti

Clafouti is a country French dessert that uses cherries. We have created a chocolate version, using cherries and plums. You can use fruit of your choice, if desired. Clafouti is an easy and colorful dish.

8 Servings

Butter-flavored, non-stick cooking spray
4–4½ cups (combined) pitted cherries and pitted purple plums, sliced (or fruit of your choice)
⅓ cup fructose (fruit sugar, see p. 3), divided
½ cup all-purpose flour
2 tablespoons unsweetened Dutch cocoa
⅛ teaspoon salt
¼ cup real egg substitute
2 egg whites, beaten
1¼ cups skim milk
1 teaspoon vanilla

Preheat oven to 350 degrees. Spray 9-inch pie plate or quiche dish. Arrange fruit in bottom of dish; sprinkle with ¼ cup fructose.

Using deep mixing bowl and whisk or food processor, combine flour, cocoa, remaining fructose, salt, egg substitute, egg whites, milk, and vanilla. Pour batter over fruit.

Bake in center of oven 1 hour or until golden brown and puffy.

Bring to table warm. You might want to sprinkle with confectioners' sugar.

Nutritional Data

PER SERVING		EXCHANGES	
Calories:	118	Milk:	0.0
% Calories from fat:	3	Veg.:	0.0
Fat (gm):	0.5	Fruit:	1.5
Sat. fat (gm):	0.1	Bread:	0.5
Cholesterol (mg):	0.6	Meat:	0.0
Sodium (mg):	84	Fat:	0.0
Protein (gm):	5		
Carbohydrate (gm):	25		

TOFU COCOA PIE

◆

Use smooth, firm tofu for a creamy pie. Do not substitute instant cocoa as it is sweetened and precooked.

8 Servings

Crust
3 chocolate graham crackers, crumbled

Filling
¼ cup dark raisins
1 tablespoon sherry or rum
1½ packets unflavored gelatin
2 cups cold water, divided
1 packet sugar-free hot cocoa mix
8 ozs. firm tofu, drained
¼ cup unsweetened Dutch cocoa
¼ cup fructose (fruit sugar, see p. 3)
1 teaspoon vanilla

Crust: Press graham cracker crumbs into bottom of pie plate. Set aside.
Filling: Put raisins in small bowl; sprinkle with sherry. Let stand until ready to use.

Stir gelatin into 1 cup water; let stand 3 to 5 minutes to dissolve. Pour into saucepan, add remaining water, and cocoa mix. Cook over medium heat until gelatin is dissolved, stirring almost constantly. Remove from heat; cool.

In food processor, combine tofu and chocolate mixture. Mix in Dutch cocoa, fructose, vanilla, and raisins with sherry.

Pour filling into pie crust. Chill until set, about 3 hours. Slice and serve.

Nutritional Data

PER SERVING		EXCHANGES	
Calories:	120	Milk:	0.0
% Calories from fat:	27	Veg.:	0.0
Fat (gm):	4	Fruit:	0.5
Sat. fat (gm):	0.8	Bread:	0.5
Cholesterol (mg):	0.2	Meat:	0.5
Sodium (mg):	56	Fat:	0.5
Protein (gm):	7		
Carbohydrate (gm):	16		

Southern Mud Pie

A crumb crust is perfect for this chilled, make-ahead pie. It's easy to prepare, and there's no crust to roll out or bake— just stir, pat, and fill.

12 Servings

Chocolate Cookie Crust
1 cup chocolate cookie crumbs (5 single cookies)
2 tablespoons diet margarine, melted
½ teaspoon ground cinnamon
¼ teaspoon ground nutmeg

Filling
1 pkg. low-calorie chocolate pudding
2 cups skim milk
1½ cups non-fat ricotta cheese
2 tablespoons fructose (fruit sugar, see p. 3)
2 tablespoons candied ginger, minced
1 tablespoon rum, or coffee liqueur
1 teaspoon chocolate sprinkles (optional)

Crust: Prepare using food processor fitted with steel blade. Combine chocolate cookie crumbs, margarine, cinnamon, and nutmeg. Pat crumbs into 9-inch pie plate.

Filling: Prepare chocolate pudding according to package directions, using skim milk. Cool until set. Spoon pudding over crust. Place in refrigerator.

Mix ricotta cheese with fructose, ginger, and rum in food processor. Puree. Spoon cheese filling over set pudding, spreading evenly over pie; mix a thin layer of chocolate into cheese. Chill until serving time.

Top with chocolate sprinkles, if desired.

Nutritional Data

PER SERVING		EXCHANGES	
Calories:	70	Milk:	0.0
% Calories from fat:	21	Veg.:	0.0
Fat (gm):	2	Fruit:	0.0
Sat. fat (gm):	0.5	Bread:	0.5
Cholesterol (mg):	4	Meat:	0.5
Sodium (mg):	79	Fat:	0.0
Protein (gm):	6		
Carbohydrate (gm):	11		

COCOA PLUM CRISP

Be sure to use ripe fruit. It will "give" when pressed gently with your finger.

9 Servings

Butter-flavored, non-stick cooking spray
4 cups ripe plums, sliced
1 teaspoon ground cinnamon
1 tablespoon sugar
2 tablespoons diet margarine, room temperature
½ cup plus 2 tablespoons quick-cooking oats, uncooked
1 tablespoon, heaping, cocoa
2 tablespoons light brown sugar

S pray an 11½ x 7-inch, non-stick pan. Preheat oven to 350 degrees. Place plums in bowl. In separate bowl, mix cinnamon with 1 tablespoon sugar; toss with plums. Arrange plums on bottom of pan.

By hand, or in electric mixer, cut margarine into small pieces. Mix together with oats, cocoa, and brown sugar. Sprinkle topping over plums.

Bake on center rack 35 minutes. Crisp will begin to brown and plums will be cooked. Spoon into shallow dishes and serve warm with low-cholesterol chocolate ice cream or whipped topping.

Nutritional Data

PER SERVING		EXCHANGES	
Calories:	116	Milk:	0.0
% Calories from fat:	12	Veg.:	0.0
Fat (gm):	2	Fruit:	1.5
Sat. fat (gm):	0.3	Bread:	0.5
Cholesterol (mg):	0	Meat:	0.0
Sodium (mg):	32	Fat:	0.0
Protein (gm):	2		
Carbohydrate (gm):	26		

4.
MOUSSES AND PUDDINGS

Chocolate Mousse

Layered Cherry-Chocolate Mousse

Old-Time Upside-Down Pudding

Cocoa Bread Pudding

Baked Chocolate Custard

Cocoa-Raisin Bread Pudding

Top-of-Stove Chocolate Custard

Chocolate Flan with Chocolate Sauce

Baked Chocolate Rice Pudding

Brown Rice and Raisin Pudding

Chocolate Pumpkin Pudding

Chocolate Indian Pudding

Chocolate Farina Pudding with Cherries

Chocolate Pudding

Chocolate Ricotta Pudding

Scandinavian Chocolate Pudding

CHOCOLATE MOUSSE

◆

In the '50s, when French chocolate mousse first became popular in America, several recipes made the rounds, including one particularly unhealthy, 2-ingredient recipe—a mixture of whipped cream and chocolate syrup.
We've created a good-tasting but much healthier alternative, using cocoa instead of chocolate and whipped topping instead of whipped cream.

◆

5 Servings, ¹/₂ cup each

¼ cup unsweetened Dutch cocoa
4 teaspoons cornstarch
1½ cups skim milk, divided
1 teaspoon vanilla extract
1½ teaspoons aspartame
1 envelope whipped topping mix

Combine cocoa and cornstarch in heavy-bottomed saucepan. Add ⅓ cup skim milk. Whisk with wire whisk until smooth.

Add another ⅔ cup milk, whisking well to combine.

Heat to boil, stirring constantly with wire whisk. Continue stirring and bring to boil. Remove from heat and allow to cool.

When cool, stir in vanilla and aspartame.

Place whipped topping in electric mixer bowl along with remaining ½ cup milk. Mix well with wire whisk. Beat according to package directions until thick. Fold whipped topping into cooled cocoa mixture.

Divide among 5 individual dishes or place in serving bowl. Refrigerate, covered, until serving time.

◆

Nutritional Data

PER SERVING		EXCHANGES	
Calories:	51	Milk:	0.5
% Calories from fat:	9	Veg.:	0.0
Fat (gm):	0.5	Fruit:	0.0
Sat. fat (gm):	0.2	Bread:	0.0
Cholesterol (mg):	1	Meat:	0.0
Sodium (mg):	42	Fat:	0.0
Protein (gm):	3		
Carbohydrate (gm):	9		

LAYERED CHERRY-CHOCOLATE MOUSSE

◆

This beautiful and delicious dessert uses both dark-colored Dutch cocoa and lighter-colored regular cocoa. Since the liquid in which canned cherries are packed differs in sweetness, be sure to taste and add additional aspartame if needed.

◆

10 Servings, 1 cup each

Dark Chocolate Mousse

1 envelope plus ¼ teaspoon unflavored gelatin
1 can (15–16 ozs.) dark cherries
Juice or syrup from cherries
½ cup water
3 tablespoons unsweetened Dutch cocoa
½ cup evaporated skim milk, at room temperature
½ teaspoon aspartame

Light Chocolate Mousse

1 envelope plus ¼ teaspoon unflavored gelatin
1 can (15–16 ozs.) light cherries
Juice or syrup from cherries
½ cup water
3 tablespoons unsweetened regular cocoa
½ cup evaporated skim milk, at room temperature
½ teaspoon aspartame

White Mousse

1 envelope plus ¼ teaspoon unflavored gelatin
Cherry juice from both cans combined with enough water to equal ¾ cup liquid
½ cup water
½ cup evaporated skim milk, at room temperature
½ teaspoon aspartame
½ teaspoon vanilla

Whipped Topping
2 envelopes whipped topping mix
1 cup skim milk, cold

Dark Chocolate Mousse: Place gelatin in small bowl. Drain dark cherries and reserve. Combine ¾ cup cherry juice with ½ cup water. Reserve remaining dark cherry juice to use with light chocolate mousse.

Spoon ¼ cup of this liquid over gelatin to soften. Heat remaining cupful to boil and add to gelatin. Stir until completely dissolved.

Place Dutch cocoa in small bowl and spoon 4 tablespoons evaporated skim milk into cocoa. Stir with wire whisk until cocoa is smooth. Add remaining skim milk and stir until smooth.

Combine cocoa and gelatin mixtures, stirring well with wire whisk. Stir in aspartame, mixing well. Cover and refrigerate.

Light Chocolate Mousse: Place gelatin in small bowl. Drain light cherries and reserve. Combine reserved dark cherry juice with enough light cherry juice to equal ¾ cup. Reserve remaining light juice to use with white mousse.

Combine ¾ cup juice with ½ cup water. Spoon ¼ cup of this liquid into gelatin to soften. Heat remaining cupful to boil and add to gelatin. Stir until completely dissolved.

Place regular cocoa in small bowl and spoon 4 tablespoons evaporated skim milk into cocoa. Stir with wire whisk until cocoa is smooth. Add remaining skim milk and stir until smooth.

Combine cocoa and gelatin mixtures, stirring well with wire whisk. Stir in aspartame. Cover and refrigerate.

White Mousse: Place gelatin in small bowl. Combine reserved light cherry juice with enough water to equal ¾ cup and combine with an additional ½ cup water.

Sprinkle ¼ cup of this liquid over gelatin to soften. Heat remaining liquid to boil and add to gelatin. Stir until completely dissolved. Stir in ½ cup evaporated skim milk, aspartame, and vanilla. Cover and refrigerate.

When all 3 mousses are partly jelled, they should be consistency of very thick egg whites. At that point, remove from refrigerator.

Chop cherries coarsely and divide into 3 sections: scant ⅔ cup dark cherries; scant ⅔ cup light cherries; and scant ⅔ cup combination light and dark cherries.

Whipped Topping: Empty two envelopes whipped topping mix into bottom of chilled electric mixer bowl. Add 1 cup cold skim milk and stir with whisk until combined. Beat according to package directions until topping stands in stiff peaks.

Layered Mousse: Use whisk to lightly beat *dark chocolate mousse.* Fold in dark cherries; then fold in 1⅓ cups whipped topping.

Spoon dark chocolate mousse into well-chilled 10 or 12-cup glass serving bowl. Cover and refrigerate.

Use whisk to lightly beat *light chocolate mousse.* Fold in ⅔ cup combination light and dark cherries; then fold in 1⅓ cups whipped topping. Cover and refrigerate.

Use whisk to beat *white mousse.* Fold in ⅔ cup light cherries; then fold in remaining 1⅓ cups whipped topping. Let stand at room temperature 1 hour.

When dark chocolate mousse is partly set, gently spoon light chocolate mousse over it. Cover and refrigerate.

After an hour, spoon white mousse over light chocolate mousse. Cover and refrigerate for at least 2 more hours before serving.

Nutritional Data

PER SERVING		EXCHANGES	
Calories:	147	Milk:	1.0
% Calories from fat:	3	Veg.:	0.0
Fat (gm):	0.5	Fruit:	1.0
Sat. fat (gm):	0.2	Bread:	0.0
Cholesterol (mg):	2	Meat:	0.0
Sodium (mg):	75	Fat:	0.0
Protein (gm):	7		
Carbohydrate (gm):	28		

OLD-TIME UPSIDE-DOWN PUDDING

The pudding is inverted after baking so that the bottom becomes the top. The pudding is covered with chocolate sauce.

8 Servings

Butter-flavored, non-stick cooking spray
1 cup all-purpose flour, sifted
2 teaspoons baking powder
¼ teaspoon each ingredient: salt, ground cinnamon
½ cup fructose (fruit sugar, see p. 3)
6 tablespoons unsweetened Dutch cocoa, divided
½ cup skim milk
1 teaspoon vanilla
2 tablespoons diet margarine, melted
½ cup dried raisins, cranberries, or cherries
½ cup, firmly packed, dark brown sugar
1¾ cups hot water

P reheat oven to 350 degrees. Spray 1½-quart baking dish.
In deep mixing bowl, combine flour, baking powder, salt, cinnamon, fructose, and 2 tablespoons cocoa. Blend in milk, vanilla, and cooled margarine. Pour mixture into prepared baking dish.

In small bowl, toss raisins, brown sugar, and remaining cocoa. Sprinkle mixture over pudding. Pour hot water evenly over pudding.

Bake on center rack of oven 40 to 50 minutes. Pudding will test done when tester inserted in center comes out dry. Cool 10 to 12 minutes. Carefully invert pudding onto deep serving dish or soup bowl. Serve immediately. You might wish to serve pudding with whipped topping.

Nutritional Data

PER SERVING		EXCHANGES	
Calories:	200	Milk:	0.0
% Calories from fat:	9	Veg.:	0.0
Fat (gm):	2	Fruit:	2.0
Sat. fat (gm):	0.4	Bread:	1.0
Cholesterol (mg):	0.3	Meat:	0.0
Sodium (mg):	197	Fat:	0.0
Protein (gm):	3		
Carbohydrate (gm):	45		

COCOA BREAD PUDDING

This recipe brings "comfort" food to a new high. It is easy to prepare and so good to taste. Stir once or twice during baking.

4 Servings

Butter-flavored, non-stick cooking spray
3 slices non-cholesterol bread
2 tablespoons golden raisins
2 cups skim milk, scalded and cooled
2 tablespoons unsweetened cocoa
½ cup real egg substitute
3 tablespoons fructose (fruit sugar, see p. 3)
1 teaspoon vanilla
¼ teaspoon chocolate extract

Preheat oven to 350 degrees. Spray a 1½-quart casserole. Remove crust from bread. Tear into 1-inch squares. Arrange bread and raisins in casserole. Set aside.

In mixing bowl, combine cooled milk with cocoa, egg substitute, fructose, vanilla, and chocolate extract. Pour milk mixture over bread and raisins.

Set casserole in larger, ovenproof pan. Fill larger pan with hot water halfway up sides of casserole. Bake 50 minutes to 1 hour. When done, a knife or bamboo skewer inserted in center of pudding will come out clean. Leave pudding in pan to cool. Can be served warm or cold.

Nutritional Data

PER SERVING		EXCHANGES	
Calories:	154	Milk:	0.5
% Calories from fat:	7	Veg.:	0.0
Fat (gm):	1	Fruit:	0.5
Sat. fat (gm):	0.4	Bread:	1.0
Cholesterol (mg):	2	Meat:	0.0
Sodium (mg):	195	Fat:	0.0
Protein (gm):	9		
Carbohydrate (gm):	28		

BAKED CHOCOLATE CUSTARD

A bain Marie is a hot water bath used for baking custard and flan. It ensures very gentle cooking and guards against overheating.

4 Servings

¼ cup sugar
½ cup real egg substitute
1½ cups skim milk
¼ cup unsweetened Dutch cocoa
½ teaspoon each ingredient: vanilla, chocolate extract
⅛ teaspoon ground cinnamon

Preheat oven to 325 degrees.

Using electric mixer, beat sugar and egg substitute until light. Mix in milk, cocoa, flavorings, and cinnamon.

Pour mixture into 4 custard cups. Place cups in baking pan. Pour hot water into pan, making a "water bath" for custard cups. Water should measure halfway up sides of cups.

Bake custard 1 hour or until knife inserted in center comes out clean. Serve custard warm or cold.

Nutritional Data

PER SERVING		EXCHANGES	
Calories:	104	Milk:	0.5
% Calories from fat:	5	Veg.:	0.0
Fat (gm):	0.7	Fruit:	0.0
Sat. fat (gm):	0.2	Bread:	1.0
Cholesterol (mg):	2	Meat:	0.0
Sodium (mg):	92	Fat:	0.0
Protein (gm):	7		
Carbohydrate (gm):	20		

COCOA-RAISIN BREAD PUDDING

This is a delicious, satisfying dish, whether served as a dessert or an "anytime" comfort food. It can be eaten hot or cold and is especially good when served with (optional) evaporated skim milk.

16 Servings

Non-stick cooking spray
- ¼ cup unsweetened Dutch cocoa
- 2½ cups skim milk, divided
- 1½ cups (12-oz. can) evaporated skim milk
- 9 tablespoons fructose (fruit sugar, see p. 3)
- 2 tablespoons diet margarine
- 4 cups coarse breadcrumbs, made from toasted, low-calorie white bread
- 1½ teaspoons cinnamon
- 1 cup real egg substitute
- ⅔ cup seedless raisins
- 16 tablespoons (1 cup) evaporated skim milk (optional)

Arrange oven rack in center of oven and preheat oven to 325 degrees. Spray 9 x 13-inch glass baking dish with non-stick cooking spray.

Place cocoa in saucepan, and stir in ¼ cup skim milk. Whisk until smooth. Stir in remaining 2¼ cups skim milk, evaporated skim milk, fructose, and margarine. Heat until margarine is melted, but do not boil.

Place breadcrumbs and cinnamon in large bowl and stir well. Pour hot milk mixture over crumbs, add egg substitute, and mix well. Stir in raisins.

Spoon batter into prepared baking dish. Bake 45 minutes or until firm. Let stand at room temperature 5 minutes.

Cut pudding into quarters; then cut each quarter into 4 pieces. Spoon one tablespoon evaporated skim milk over each helping, if desired.

Nutritional Data

PER SERVING		EXCHANGES	
Calories:	116	Milk:	0.5
% Calories from fat:	11	Veg.:	0.0
Fat (gm):	1	Fruit:	0.5
Sat. fat (gm):	0.3	Bread:	0.5
Cholesterol (mg):	2	Meat:	0.0
Sodium (mg):	143	Fat:	0.0
Protein (gm):	6		
Carbohydrate (gm):	21		

TOP-OF-STOVE CHOCOLATE CUSTARD

To make vanilla custard, omit the cocoa and chocolate extract and increase vanilla to ³/₄ teaspoon.
Custard is a favorite of all ages. It is either gently cooked on top of the stove or baked until firm. Either way, it is creamy and smooth.

4 Servings

- 3 tablespoons fructose (fruit sugar, see p. 3)
- ¼ cup cornstarch
- ¼ cup unsweetened Dutch cocoa
- 2 cups skim milk
- ½ cup real egg substitute
- ½ teaspoon each ingredient: vanilla, chocolate extract

Using small, heavy saucepan (or top of double-boiler over simmering water), mix fructose, cornstarch, and cocoa. Whisk in skim milk, egg substitute, and flavorings. Continue cooking over medium-low heat about 8 minutes or until custard is thick; it should be able to coat back of dipped spoon.

Pour custard evenly into 4 shallow dishes or custard cups. Chill 2 to 3 hours or until custard is set. Serve as is or unmold onto serving dish.

Nutritional Data

PER SERVING		EXCHANGES	
Calories:	128	Milk:	1.0
% Calories from fat:	5	Veg.:	0.0
Fat (gm):	0.7	Fruit:	0.0
Sat. fat (gm):	0.3	Bread:	0.5
Cholesterol (mg):	2	Meat:	0.5
Sodium (mg):	108	Fat:	0.0
Protein (gm):	8		
Carbohydrate (gm):	24		

CHOCOLATE FLAN WITH CHOCOLATE SAUCE

◆

Many thanks to our Mexican counterparts for this recipe. Flan has long been a classic south of the border. Since chocolate is native to Mexico, this recipe is a natural blend.

◆

6 Servings

Sugar Topping
¼ cup sugar
1 teaspoon water

Flan
1 can (12 ozs.) evaporated skim milk
½ cup skim milk
¾ cup real egg substitute
2 tablespoons cocoa
¼ cup fructose (fruit sugar, see p. 3)
¾ teaspoon vanilla
¼ teaspoon chocolate extract
Chocolate Sauce (recipe follows)

Preheat oven to 325 degrees. Use 1-quart metal ring mold.

Topping: In small, heavy saucepan, cook sugar with 1 teaspoon water over medium heat until syrup becomes golden color. Stir occasionally, being careful not to burn sugar. Working quickly, pour syrup into metal ring mold. Using potholders, tip mold from side to side so that sugar is evenly distributed on bottom of mold. Set aside to harden.

Flan: In medium saucepan, combine evaporated skim milk and skim milk. Scald and cool. In separate pan, heat and whisk together egg substitute with cocoa, fructose, vanilla, and chocolate extract. Slowly pour milk into cocoa mixture. Transfer Flan to ring mold.

Set ring mold in large pan and pour hot water halfway up side of mold. Bake 65 to 75 minutes or until tester or bamboo skewer inserted in center of flan comes out clean. Remove from oven, cool, and refrigerate 3 hours.

Prepare Chocolate Sauce while Flan is refrigerating.

Using knife, loosen edges of flan. Invert it onto serving dish. Spoon 2 tablespoons Chocolate Sauce over each flan serving.

Chocolate Sauce

Makes 1 cup & 2 tablespoons

1 can (12 ozs.) evaporated skim milk
3 tablespoons cocoa
⅓ cup fructose (fruit sugar, see p. 3)
2 tablespoons cornstarch
1 teaspoon vanilla
½ teaspoon chocolate extract
2 tablespoons rum, or chocolate liqueur

In small, heavy saucepan, scald milk. Stir in cocoa and fructose. Simmer until fructose dissolves.

Remove ¼ cup of sauce; whisk in cornstarch. Simmer, stirring cornstarch, until sauce thickens slightly, 1 to 2 minutes. Remove from heat; stir in vanilla, chocolate extract, and liqueur. Place in covered container and refrigerate until needed. Serve hot or cold.

Nutritional Data

PER SERVING		EXCHANGES	
Calories:	124	Milk:	0.5
% Calories from fat:	2	Veg.:	0.0
Fat (gm):	0.3	Fruit:	0.0
Sat. fat (gm):	0.1	Bread:	1.0
Cholesterol (mg):	3	Meat:	0.0
Sodium (mg):	118	Fat:	0.0
Protein (gm):	8		
Carbohydrate (gm):	23		

BAKED CHOCOLATE RICE PUDDING

Only a small amount of rice is used in this recipe. It gives custard pudding both body and taste and is a good use for leftover cooked plain rice.

6 Servings

Butter-flavored, non-stick cooking spray
¼ cup real egg substitute
2 egg whites
¼ cup unsweetened Dutch cocoa
⅓ cup fructose (fruit sugar, see p. 3)
2 cups skim milk
1 cup cooked plain rice
½ teaspoon ground cinnamon
¼ teaspoon salt
1 teaspoon vanilla

P reheat oven to 375 degrees. Spray 2-quart ovenproof dish.
Whisk together egg substitute and egg whites in large bowl. In separate bowl, mix cocoa with fructose; add to eggs. Continue beating until incorporated. Mix in milk. Stir in rice, cinnamon, salt, and vanilla.

Pour rice mixture into prepared baking dish.

Place a pan, larger than bowl, on middle rack in oven. Position dish in pan, and fill pan with hot water reaching two-thirds up sides of dish. Bake pudding, uncovered, 1 hour or until custard is set and knife when inserted in custard, comes out clean. Stir once or twice during cooking.

Cool. Spoon custard into small dessert cups. Serve with whipped topping, if desired.

Nutritional Data

PER SERVING		EXCHANGES	
Calories:	125	Milk:	0.0
% Calories from fat:	4	Veg.:	0.0
Fat (gm):	0.6	Fruit:	0.5
Sat. fat (gm):	0.2	Bread:	1.0
Cholesterol (mg):	1	Meat:	0.5
Sodium (mg):	166	Fat:	0.0
Protein (gm):	6		
Carbohydrate (gm):	24		

BROWN RICE AND RAISIN PUDDING

To cook brown rice, bring 1¾ cups of water to boil. Add 1 cup brown rice. Cover. Simmer 30 minutes or until rice is tender.

8 Servings

2 cups cooked brown rice, set aside
   Butter-flavored, non-stick cooking spray
3 cups skim milk
¼ cup unsweetened Dutch cocoa
1 cup real egg substitute
⅛ teaspoon salt
¼ cup fructose (fruit sugar, see p. 3)
1 teaspoon ground cinnamon
1 teaspoon vanilla
½ teaspoon chocolate extract
⅓ cup golden raisins
2 egg whites, beaten

P reheat oven to 350 degrees. Spray 1½-quart casserole.

Mix together milk, cocoa, egg substitute, salt, fructose, cinnamon, vanilla, chocolate extract, and raisins. Add rice. Fold in beaten egg whites.

Pour into prepared casserole. Place in oven in larger pan, with hot water reaching halfway up sides of casserole. Bake 50 to 60 minutes or until knife inserted in pudding comes out clean. Serve warm.

If top of pudding begins to get too brown, cover with aluminum foil.

Nutritional Data

PER SERVING		EXCHANGES	
Calories:	134	Milk:	0.0
% Calories from fat:	6	Veg.:	0.0
Fat (gm):	0.9	Fruit:	0.5
Sat. fat (gm):	0.2	Bread:	1.0
Cholesterol (mg):	1	Meat:	0.5
Sodium (mg):	129	Fat:	0.0
Protein (gm):	8		
Carbohydrate (gm):	25		

CHOCOLATE PUMPKIN PUDDING

The chocolate flavor in this unusual, good-tasting pudding is so delicate that it functions more as an undertaste than as a predominant flavor.

12 Servings

Butter-flavored, non-stick cooking spray
4   teaspoons unsweetened Dutch cocoa
1   teaspoon cinnamon
½   teaspoon allspice
¼   teaspoon nutmeg
⅛   teaspoon ginger
1⅔ cups evaporated skim milk
1   cup real egg substitute
¾   cup plus 2 tablespoons fructose (fruit sugar, see p. 3)
1   can (16 ozs.) pumpkin

Adjust oven rack to center of oven and preheat oven to 350 degrees. Spray 10-inch pie pan or 10-inch shallow, ovenproof casserole with non-stick cooking spray.

Combine cocoa, cinnamon, allspice, nutmeg, and ginger in small bowl, and stir in a few spoonfuls of evaporated skim milk. Work mixture to smooth paste with wire whisk.

Add a few additional spoonfuls until mixture is liquid. Add remaining evaporated milk. Stir with whisk if mixture seems lumpy; or put through strainer.

Place egg substitute in electric mixer bowl and beat until foamy. Add fructose and beat again. Then beat in pumpkin, mixing well. Add cocoa/milk mixture and beat again.

Spoon pudding into prepared pan. Bake 1 hour. Remove from oven and serve, or allow to cool first.

Nutritional Data

PER SERVING		EXCHANGES	
Calories:	120	Milk:	0.0
% Calories from fat:	1	Veg.:	0.0
Fat (gm):	0.2	Fruit:	0.0
Sat. fat (gm):	0.1	Bread:	1.5
Cholesterol (mg):	1	Meat:	0.0
Sodium (mg):	148	Fat:	0.0
Protein (gm):	5		
Carbohydrate (gm):	25		

CHOCOLATE INDIAN PUDDING

This absolutely delicious pudding has a faint chocolate flavor. But if you like a more intense chocolate taste, increase the cocoa by 1 or 2 tablespoons. If pudding becomes too thick or if you wish to reheat it, use a wire whisk to stir in additional skim milk. Reheat pudding in a double-boiler.

8 Servings, ⅓ cup each

Butter-flavored, non-stick cooking spray
2 tablespoons unsweetened Dutch cocoa
4⅔ cups skim milk, divided
6 tablespoons cornmeal
6 tablespoons fructose (fruit sugar, see p. 3)
¼ teaspoon baking soda
1 teaspoon ginger
1 teaspoon cinnamon
6 tablespoons molasses
Nutmeg, large pinch
8 tablespoons evaporated skim milk (optional)

djust rack to center of oven and preheat oven to 275 degrees. Spray shallow, 6-cup ovenproof casserole with non-stick cooking spray.

Place cocoa in small bowl and add ⅓ cup skim milk. Stir with wire whisk until very smooth.

Heat 3 cups milk in heavy-bottomed saucepan and stir in cornmeal. Cook over low heat, stirring constantly until thick, about 12 minutes.

Stir cocoa paste into cornmeal mixture, along with fructose baking soda, ginger, and cinnamon, mixing well. Then stir in molasses and remaining 1⅓ cups skim milk.

Spoon pudding into prepared casserole, and bake 90 to 100 minutes or until very thick but not solid. (If pudding gets too thick, stir in a little additional skim milk.) As pudding bakes, use spoon every 30 to 40 minutes to stir skin back into pudding.

Remove casserole from oven and sprinkle with nutmeg. Bring hot casserole to table. Serve with optional pitcher of evaporated skim milk to pour over each serving as desired.

Nutritional Data

PER SERVING		EXCHANGES	
Calories:	138	Milk:	1.0
% Calories from fat:	3	Veg.:	0.0
Fat (gm):	0.5	Fruit:	1.0
Sat. fat (gm):	0.2	Bread:	0.0
Cholesterol (mg):	2	Meat:	0.0
Sodium (mg):	115	Fat:	0.0
Protein (gm):	6		
Carbohydrate (gm):	28		

CHOCOLATE FARINA PUDDING WITH CHERRIES

This very delicious pudding is quick and easy to make. If desired, serve it with whipped topping made with 1 envelope whipped topping mix and ½ cup cold skim milk.

9 Servings

Butter-flavored, non-stick cooking spray
1 can (16 ozs.) dark cherries
3 cups skim milk (or enough to increase canned cherry juice to 4 cups)
6 tablespoons unsweetened Dutch cocoa
½ cup fructose (fruit sugar, see p. 3)
½ cup farina

Spray 8 x 4-inch bread pan with non-stick cooking spray. Drain cherries, measure juice, and add enough skim milk to measure 4 cups combined liquid. Set cherries aside.

Place cocoa in saucepan and add ½ cup juice/milk mixture. Cook over low heat, stirring constantly with wire whisk until cocoa is incorporated. Add remaining juice/milk mixture and mix well.

Stir in fructose and heat to boil. Lower heat and stir in farina. Simmer, stirring often with wire whisk until farina is cooked and mixture is very thick. Stir in whole cherries.

Spoon pudding into prepared bread pan and press lightly to pack into mold. Smooth top with spatula. Cover with wax paper and chill at least 5 hours in refrigerator.

At serving time, run thin-bladed knife around pudding to loosen it from pan. Turn out onto serving platter and remove wax paper. Use sharp knife to cut into 9 slices (each a scant 1-inch).

If desired, make whipped topping according to package directions and top each slice with a few spoonfuls.

Nutritional Data

PER SERVING		EXCHANGES	
Calories:	138	Milk:	0.5
% Calories from fat:	4	Veg.:	0.0
Fat (gm):	0.6	Fruit:	1.0
Sat. fat (gm):	0.2	Bread:	0.5
Cholesterol (mg):	1	Meat:	0.0
Sodium (mg):	46	Fat:	0.0
Protein (gm):	5		
Carbohydrate (gm):	30		

CHOCOLATE PUDDING

This pudding is delicious and well within most dieters' calorie and fat budgets.

4 Servings, ½ cup each

1 teaspoon gelatin
2 teaspoons water
3 tablespoons unsweetened Dutch cocoa
3 tablespoons cornstarch
2 cups skim milk, divided
1 teaspoon vanilla
3½ teaspoons aspartame

P lace gelatin in top of small double-boiler and sprinkle water on to soften. Melt over simmering water.

Combine cocoa and cornstarch in heavy-bottomed saucepan. Add ⅓ cup skim milk and mix with whisk until smooth and soft. Add remaining milk, a little at a time, until well incorporated.

Heat to boil, stirring constantly. Boil 1 minute, stirring constantly, and remove from heat. Add melted gelatin to pudding and stir to combine.

Cool slightly, then stir in vanilla and aspartame.

Divide among 4 serving bowls. Cover and refrigerate until serving time.

Nutritional Data

PER SERVING		EXCHANGES	
Calories:	82	Milk:	0.5
% Calories from fat:	6	Veg.:	0.0
Fat (gm):	0.6	Fruit:	0.0
Sat. fat (gm):	0.2	Bread:	0.5
Cholesterol (mg):	2	Meat:	0.0
Sodium (mg):	67	Fat:	0.0
Protein (gm):	6		
Carbohydrate (gm):	15		

CHOCOLATE RICOTTA PUDDING

This classic Italian pudding is made with ricotta cheese, confectioners' sugar, and rum. We added the cocoa but lowered fat and calories by using low-fat ricotta and aspartame. If you wish, lower calories still further by using no-fat ricotta. Orange liqueur can also be substituted for the rum with excellent results.

8 Servings, about ⅓ cup each

1½ tablespoons unsweetened Dutch cocoa
3   tablespoons rum
2⅔ cups low-fat ricotta cheese
3½ teaspoons aspartame
    Large pinch unsweetened Dutch cocoa
    Large pinch aspartame

Combine cocoa and rum and stir until smooth. Add mixture to ricotta. Add aspartame and stir together well.

Spoon pudding into glass bowl. Cover and chill 3 hours or more. Mix a large pinch each of cocoa and aspartame and sprinkle over pudding. Divide pudding among 8 dessert bowls.

Nutritional Data

PER SERVING		EXCHANGES	
Calories:	83	Milk:	0.0
% Calories from fat:	24	Veg.:	0.0
Fat (gm):	2	Fruit:	0.0
Sat. fat (gm):	trace	Bread:	0.5
Cholesterol (mg):	11	Meat:	1.0
Sodium (mg):	61	Fat:	0.0
Protein (gm):	8		
Carbohydrate (gm):	5		

SCANDINAVIAN CHOCOLATE PUDDING

In Scandinavian countries such as Finland, this satisfying and hearty chocolate farina is served as either a dessert or a breakfast.

5 Servings, about 2¼ cups

- 2 cups skim milk, divided
- 4 teaspoons unsweetened Dutch cocoa
- ⅓ cup farina
- ½ teaspoon vanilla
- 1¾ teaspoons aspartame

P lace all but 2 or 3 tablespoons of milk in heavy-bottomed saucepan. Place cocoa in medium bowl and add 2 or 3 tablespoons milk. Stir with wire whisk until smooth.

Heat milk in saucepan to just below boiling point. Scrape cocoa paste into hot milk, and stir with whisk until well mixed. Add farina and cook over low heat, stirring constantly, until thickened, about 3 minutes.

Remove from heat and allow to cool slightly. Stir in vanilla and aspartame sweetener. Divide pudding among 5 serving dishes and serve immediately.

Nutritional Data

PER SERVING		EXCHANGES	
Calories:	83	Milk:	0.5
% Calories from fat:	4	Veg.:	0.0
Fat (gm):	0.4	Fruit:	0.0
Sat. fat (gm):	0.2	Bread:	0.5
Cholesterol (mg):	2	Meat:	0.0
Sodium (mg):	52	Fat:	0.0
Protein (gm):	5		
Carbohydrate (gm):	15		

5.

CREPES, PANCAKES, AND NOODLES

Chocolate Crepes with Cherries

Mount Crepe

Chocolate Crepes with Chèvre Cheese and Strawberries

Chocolate Blintzes

Chocolate Potato Waffles

Scandinavian Pancakes with Lingonberries

Rolled Dessert Pancakes

Chocolate Fettuccine Noodles

Chocolate Fettuccine with Ricotta and Orange

Chocolate Fettuccine with Yogurt and Raspberries

Chocolate Noodles with Apples and Cinnamon

CHOCOLATE CREPES WITH CHERRIES

Let batter stand 20 minutes before cooking. The flour will be absorbed, and a more even crepe will result. If the crepe batter becomes too thick, add water by the tablespoon until it reaches the desired thickness.

10 Servings, 1 crepe each

- 1½ cups cake flour
- ¼ cup unsweetened Dutch cocoa
- 1 cup skim milk
- ¼ cup real egg substitute
- 1 egg white
- 2 tablespoons sugar
- 2 tablespoons diet margarine, melted
- Butter-flavored, non-stick cooking spray, or 2 teaspoons light margarine
- **Sauce** (recipe follows)

I n large, deep bowl or food processor, blend together flour, cocoa, milk, egg substitute, egg white, sugar, and melted margarine. Let stand 20 minutes.

Spray 6-inch, non-stick frying pan or crepe pan (or use small amount of margarine). With ladle, pour about 3 tablespoons of batter into hot pan. Swirl evenly in pan. Pour off excess batter after pan bottom is covered with batter.

Cook crepe over medium heat until bottom is cooked. Turn crepe over and continue cooking until done. Invert crepe on clean kitchen towel. Continue until all crepes are done. When cool, stack crepes with sheets of waxed paper between them.

Sauce
1 cup "all fruit" spreadable jam, black cherry
2 tablespoons sweet red wine, or cherry liqueur
⅛ teaspoon ground cardamon
1 can (15 ozs.) red cherries, drained, reserve juice

Heat jam with 2 tablespoons red wine or cherry liqueur and 2 tablespoons water. Mix in cardamon. Mix with cherries and ½ cup cherry juice.

To Assemble: Set crepe on plate, spoon 1½ tablespoons sauce over top, and fold once each way. Drizzle with sauce and cherries.

Nutritional Data

PER SERVING		EXCHANGES	
Calories:	208	Milk:	0.0
% Calories from fat:	7	Veg.:	0.0
Fat (gm):	2	Fruit:	1.0
Sat. fat (gm):	0.3	Bread:	2.0
Cholesterol (mg):	0.4	Meat:	0.0
Sodium (mg):	59	Fat:	0.0
Protein (gm):	4		
Carbohydrate (gm):	46		

MOUNT CREPE

◆

The "mount" is a stack of 10 crepes with layers of peach-cheese filling between them. It is then cut like a pie.

◆

8 Servings

1½ cups cake flour
¼ cup cocoa
1 cup skim milk
¼ cup real egg substitute
1 egg white
2 teaspoons fructose (fruit sugar, see p. 3)
2 tablespoons diet margarine, melted
  Butter-flavored, non-stick cooking spray
  Filling (recipe follows)

I n large, deep bowl or food processor, blend together flour, cocoa, milk, egg substitute, egg white, fructose, and melted margarine. Let stand 20 minutes.

Spray 10-inch, non-stick frying pan. With ladle, pour about 5 tablespoons batter into hot pan. Swirl batter evenly in pan. Pour off excess batter after pan bottom is covered with batter.

Cook crepe over medium heat until bottom is cooked. Turn crepe over and continue cooking until done. Invert crepe on clean kitchen towel. Continue until all crepes are done. While crepes are cooling, prepare Filling.

Filling

1¼ lbs. non-fat ricotta cheese, or skim cottage cheese
⅓ cup non-fat vanilla yogurt
1 can, (8 ozs.) thin peach slices, drained, reserve 2 tablespoons juice
1 teaspoon aspartame

In large bowl, mix cheese, yogurt, and peaches (reserve 3 slices for top of mount). Mash peaches as you mix filling, adding aspartame and enough juice from peaches to make a smooth filling.

To Assemble: Set first crepe in center of serving dish. Spread lightly with filling. Continue until all crepes have been stacked. Top with final layer of peach-cheese filling, and place remaining peach slices on top. You can arrange top slices in flower shape for elegance.

Slice crepe "mount" carefully with sharp or serrated knife into 8 servings.

Nutritional Data

PER SERVING		EXCHANGES	
Calories:	181	Milk:	0.0
% Calories from fat:	14	Veg.:	0.0
Fat (gm):	3	Fruit:	0.5
Sat. fat (gm):	0.7	Bread:	1.0
Cholesterol (mg):	8	Meat:	1.5
Sodium (mg):	112	Fat:	0.0
Protein (gm):	15		
Carbohydrate (gm):	32		

CHOCOLATE CREPES WITH CHÈVRE CHEESE AND STRAWBERRIES

A delightful combination! Chocolate crepes add a new dimension to desserts. Be creative and add your own filling if this one holds no appeal.

10 Servings, 1 crepe each

- 1½ cups cake flour
- ¼ cup unsweetened Dutch cocoa
- 1 cup skim milk
- 1 egg
- 1 egg white
- 2 tablespoons sugar
- 2 tablespoons diet margarine, melted, cooled
  Butter-flavored, non-stick cooking spray, or 2 teaspoons diet margarine
  Filling (recipe follows)
  Sauce (recipe follows)

I n large, deep bowl or food processor, blend together flour, cocoa, milk, egg, egg white, sugar, and melted margarine. Let stand 20 minutes. Meanwhile, prepare filling.

Spray a 6-inch, non-stick frying pan or crepe pan (or use small amount of margarine). With ladle, pour about 3 tablespoons of batter into hot pan. Swirl evenly into pan. Pour off excess batter after pan bottom is covered with batter.

Cook crepe over medium heat until bottom is cooked. Turn crepe over and continue cooking until done. Invert crepe on clean kitchen towel.

Continue until all crepes are done. When cool, stack crepes with sheets of waxed paper between them.

Filling

½ lb. plain goat's (Chèvre) cheese
½ lb. non-fat ricotta, or skim cottage cheese
½ cup no-fat sour cream
2 cups sliced strawberries
3 tablespoons fructose (fruit sugar, see p. 3), or to taste

Mix together cheeses with sour cream, strawberries, and fructose to taste.

To fill, spoon 2 tablespoons Filling down center of each crepe, roll up, and place on plate.

Sauce

2 cups sliced strawberries
2 teaspoons aspartame (white or brown)

Toss strawberries with aspartame to make sauce. Spoon onto crepes and serve immediately.

◆

Nutritional Data

PER SERVING		EXCHANGES	
Calories:	198	Milk:	0.0
% Calories from fat:	27	Veg.:	0.0
Fat (gm):	6	Fruit:	0.5
Sat. fat (gm):	4	Bread:	1.5
Cholesterol (mg):	44	Meat:	1.0
Sodium (mg):	139	Fat:	0.0
Protein (gm):	11		
Carbohydrate (gm):	28		

CHOCOLATE BLINTZES

If your pan is well seasoned, it may not be necessary to spray pan before preparing each crepe.

12 Servings, 1 blintz each

¼ cup real egg substitute

2 egg whites

1 cup, scant, all-purpose flour

3 tablespoons unsweetened Dutch cocoa

½ cup water

½ cup skim milk

2 tablespoons diet margarine, melted, cooled

2 tablespoons sugar

Butter-flavored, non-stick cooking spray, or 2 teaspoons diet margarine

3 tablespoons diet margarine

Filling (recipe follows)

In large, deep bowl or food processor, blend together egg substitute, egg whites, flour, cocoa, water, milk, cooled margarine, and sugar. Let batter stand 20 minutes.

Spray 5- or 6-inch, non-stick frying pan or crepe pan. With ladle, pour about 3 tablespoons batter onto hot pan. Swish batter evenly in pan, covering bottom. Pour off excess batter after pan bottom is covered.

Cook blintz over medium heat until bottom is cooked. Turn blintz over and continue cooking until done. Invert blintz on clean kitchen towel. Continue until all blintzes are done. While blintzes are cooling, prepare Filling.

Filling

1 lb. light farmer's cheese, or skim cottage cheese
½ cup non-fat vanilla yogurt
¼ cup sugar
3 tablespoons fructose (fruit sugar, see p. 3)
¼ teaspoon salt

In deep bowl, combine cheese, yogurt, sugar, fructose, and salt.

To Assemble: Spoon about 1½ tablespoons filling down center of blintz. Fold over both sides and bring up both ends (envelope style). Place blintz seam side down on lightly floured plate until serving time.

To Serve: When ready to serve, melt margarine in non-stick frying pan. Cook blintzes until lightly browned on both sides. Serve immediately. You might want to serve with small amount of chocolate sauce or sprinkle of confectioners' sugar.

Nutritional Data

PER SERVING		EXCHANGES	
Calories:	144	Milk:	0.0
% Calories from fat:	28	Veg.:	0.0
Fat (gm):	5	Fruit:	0.0
Sat. fat (gm):	0.5	Bread:	1.0
Cholesterol (mg):	5	Meat:	0.5
Sodium (mg):	138	Fat:	1.0
Protein (gm):	6		
Carbohydrate (gm):	21		

CHOCOLATE POTATO WAFFLES

Ginger-yogurt topping gives these waffles a very special flavor.

4 Servings, 1 waffle each

¾ cup all-purpose flour
3 tablespoons cocoa
2 teaspoons fructose (fruit sugar, see p. 3)
1½ teaspoons baking powder
½ teaspoon baking soda
¼ teaspoon salt
2 egg whites
4 teaspoons diet margarine, melted, cooled
1 cup buttermilk
1 cup cooked mashed potatoes
Butter-flavored, non-stick cooking spray
1 cup vanilla non-fat yogurt
1 tablespoon candied ginger

S ift flour, cocoa, fructose, baking powder, baking soda, and salt into large bowl.

In electric mixer bowl, lightly beat egg whites. Beat in cooled margarine and buttermilk. Add flour/cocoa mixture and potatoes.

Heat a sprayed waffle iron. Pour ¼ cup waffle mixture into center of waffle iron. Cook until brown, according to manufacturer's directions.

In small bowl, combine yogurt and ginger for topping.

Place waffles on individual plates and top each with tablespoon of ginger-yogurt. Serve hot.

Nutritional Data

PER SERVING		EXCHANGES	
Calories:	203	Milk:	0.0
% Calories from fat:	14	Veg.:	0.0
Fat (gm):	3	Fruit:	0.0
Sat. fat (gm):	1	Bread:	2.5
Cholesterol (mg):	4	Meat:	0.0
Sodium (mg):	798	Fat:	0.5
Protein (gm):	9		
Carbohydrate (gm):	37		

SCANDINAVIAN PANCAKES WITH LINGONBERRIES

Scandinavian pancakes are delicate cocoa-flavored morsels served with either lingonberries or raspberries. There is a special pan for these pancakes; it has circular depressions for the pancakes so all are one size. But we just use a large, non-stick frying pan. Lingonberry sauce is available in large supermarkets and at Scandinavian grocery stores.

8 Servings

¼ cup real egg substitute
2 egg whites, beaten
2 cups skim milk
2 tablespoons diet margarine, melted
1½ cups all-purpose flour
3 tablespoons cocoa
2 tablespoons fructose (fruit sugar, see p. 3)
¼ teaspoon salt
⅛ teaspoon ground cardamon
  Butter-flavored, non-stick cooking spray
1 cup prepared lingonberry sauce, or 2 cups raspberries
1¾ teaspoons aspartame, or to taste
3 tablespoons orange juice, freshly squeezed

B eat egg substitute in large bowl of electric mixer. Add beaten egg whites. Stir in milk and margarine.

Sift together flour, cocoa, fructose, salt, and cardamon. (We sift through a large strainer onto a paper plate.) Mix sifted ingredients into egg mixture. Let batter stand 15 to 20 minutes.

Spray and heat a large, non-stick frying pan. Drop 1 heaping tablespoon batter for each pancake; pancakes will be about 2½ inches round. Continue cooking over medium heat until pancakes are firm and golden brown on bottom. Using spatula, turn pancakes and cook until lightly brown on both sides. Serve hot with lingonberry or raspberry sauce.

To prepare raspberry sauce, wash, drain, and place berries in saucepan. Stir in orange juice. Cook over medium heat until hot, 3 to 5 minutes, stirring often. Cool slightly; mix in aspartame and pour into sauce bowl.

Nutritional Data

PER SERVING		EXCHANGES	
Calories:	154	Milk:	0.5
% Calories from fat:	12	Veg.:	0.0
Fat (gm):	2	Fruit:	0.5
Sat. fat (gm):	0.4	Bread:	1.0
Cholesterol (mg):	1	Meat:	0.0
Sodium (mg):	156	Fat:	0.5
Protein (gm):	7		
Carbohydrate (gm):	27		

ROLLED DESSERT PANCAKES

You might wish to sprinkle pancakes with confectioners' sugar before serving. It makes a lovely presentation.

8 Servings

- 2 cups cooked mashed potatoes, cold
- ½ teaspoon ground cinnamon
- ¼ teaspoon each ingredient: ground mace, salt
- ½ cup all-purpose flour
  Butter-flavored, non-stick cooking spray
- 1 tablespoon diet margarine
- 8 teaspoons low-calorie raspberry or strawberry jam

I n mixing bowl, combine cold mashed potatoes, cinnamon, mace, salt, and flour. Knead dough to make sure all ingredients are well blended.

Divide dough into 8 equal pieces. Knead each piece into ball; roll balls out thinly on lightly floured surface. It is a good idea to use a cloth surface and a sleeve on rolling pin.

Spray well-seasoned, non-stick frying pan. Melt margarine in pan. Using spatula, transfer 1 pancake to pan; cook over medium heat until golden brown on bottom. Turn once with spatula and continue cooking until pancake is done on both sides. If bubbles form during cooking, pierce with fork.

Spread each pancake with 1 teaspoon jam. Roll up pancake. Place it seam down on dessert dish and serve hot. If you prepare pancakes before serving time, reheat them in 275-degree oven, if necessary.

Nutritional Data

PER SERVING		EXCHANGES	
Calories:	84	Milk:	0.0
% Calories from fat:	12	Veg.:	0.0
Fat (gm):	1	Fruit:	0.0
Sat. fat (gm):	0.3	Bread:	1.0
Cholesterol (mg):	1	Meat:	0.0
Sodium (mg):	248	Fat:	0.0
Protein (gm):	2		
Carbohydrate (gm):	17		

CHOCOLATE FETTUCCINE NOODLES

This unusual chocolate noodle recipe serves as the base for several chocolate noodle desserts (see following). Or, if you prefer, simply boil, drain, and serve them, hot or cold, tossed with peeled, chopped apple slices, fresh raspberries, or hulled strawberries.

6 Servings

1⅔ cups unsifted flour
⅓ cup unsweetened Dutch cocoa
1 tablespoon fructose (fruit sugar, see p. 3)
½ cup real egg substitute
1 tablespoon salad oil
1 tablespoon water, plus additional as needed

To Make by Hand: Sift flour, cocoa, and fructose together into large bowl. Make a well in center of mixture and add egg substitute, oil, and 1 tablespoon water.

Mix dough together with fingers, adding a few drops of water as necessary, to form a ball. Knead ball a few times. If ball is so dry that scraps and bits of dough fall off or flour cannot all be incorporated, add more water, a few drops at a time, until ball can be kneaded.

Knead dough until smooth and elastic, 15 to 20 minutes, adding additional flour if dough seems sticky or drops of water if it seems dry. Let dough rest 10 minutes before rolling out.

Lightly flour a large cloth. Divide dough into 2 equal-size balls. Use rolling pin to roll one ball lengthwise. Then roll dough widthwise. Continue rolling in alternate directions until dough is paper thin. If dough sticks at any time during rolling, loosen it gently with spatula and flour it lightly underneath. Repeat with remaining ball of dough.

Carefully roll each flat of dough into cylinder, as you would for jellyroll. Slice roll crosswise into even coils, ¼ inch wide. Unroll coils and place them on lightly floured tray until all noodles have been cut.

Use noodles in following recipes. Or wrap them tightly in plastic wrap and store in refrigerator up to 48 hours.

To Make by Machine: Place all ingredients in food processor. Pulse until ingredients are very well mixed.

Remove dough from processor and form into ball. If ingredients are too dry, add water, a few drops at a time, until ball forms easily. If ingredients are sticky, add a few sprinkles of flour and knead into ball.

Divide dough into 12 portions. Set smooth rollers of pasta machine on widest setting. Feed dough, one portion at a time, through setting until dough is smooth and elastic. This may take a dozen or more times for each portion of dough (chocolate pasta takes more kneading than plain pasta), but each pass takes only a few seconds. If any portion of dough resists the rollers or rolling out, flour it lightly on both sides. Let dough rest 10 minutes after kneading.

Set smooth rollers on second notch and feed dough through on this setting. Set rollers on third notch and feed each portion through rollers as before. Continue narrowing settings until first portion of dough passes through setting 6.

Cut fettuccine noodles by feeding first dough portion through wide cutting blades of pasta machine. Immediately separate noodles. If noodles will not separate easily, lightly flour each portion of dough before feeding it through wide cutting blades.

Arrange noodles separately on tray. Continue feeding each dough portion, one at a time, through setting 6 and then through wide noodle cutting blade.

Use noodles immediately in following recipes. Or wrap them tightly in plastic wrap and refrigerate up to 48 hours.

Nutritional Data

PER SERVING		EXCHANGES	
Calories:	171	Milk:	0.0
% Calories from fat:	16	Veg.:	0.0
Fat (gm):	3	Fruit:	0.0
Sat. fat (gm):	0.5	Bread:	2.0
Cholesterol (mg):	0	Meat:	0.0
Sodium (mg):	31	Fat:	0.5
Protein (gm):	6		
Carbohydrate (gm):	31		

CHOCOLATE FETTUCCINE WITH RICOTTA AND ORANGE

This chocolate fettuccine is chilled, then tossed with orange-flavored ricotta cheese and fresh orange segments.

10 Servings, about ¾ cup each

4 qts. water
1 recipe Chocolate Fettuccine Noodles (preceding)
1 can (15 ozs.) mandarin orange segments, chilled (or substitute 30 small, freshly peeled orange segments)
2½ cups low-fat ricotta cheese
1 tablespoon aspartame
2 teaspoons orange rind, freshly grated
2–3 tablespoons orange liqueur

Heat water to boil. Add noodles and cook 5 minutes or until tender. Drain noodles in collander and run cold tap water over to stop cooking. Shake collander to remove excess water. Transfer to covered casserole or plastic bag. Chill in refrigerator.

Drain orange segments in collander.

Combine ricotta, aspartame, orange rind, and orange liqueur in small bowl.

Place chilled fettuccine in glass bowl and toss with ricotta mixture. Fold in orange segments. Serve immediately.

Nutritional Data

PER SERVING		EXCHANGES	
Calories:	180	Milk:	0.0
% Calories from fat:	17	Veg.:	0.0
Fat (gm):	3	Fruit:	0.5
Sat. fat (gm):	0.3	Bread:	1.0
Cholesterol (mg):	8	Meat:	1.0
Sodium (mg):	66	Fat:	0.5
Protein (gm):	10		
Carbohydrate (gm):	27		

CHOCOLATE FETTUCCINE WITH YOGURT AND RASPBERRIES

This unusual dish will elicit raves from your guests. Substitute strawberries for raspberries, or use both berries if desired.

10 Servings, ½ cup each

- 4 qts. water
- 1 recipe Chocolate Fettuccine Noodles (preceding)
- 3⅓ cups non-fat vanilla yogurt, aspartame sweetened
- 1¼ cups (20 tablespoons) fresh raspberries

Heat water to boil in large pot. Add noodles and cook 5 minutes or until tender. Drain in collander and run cold water over to stop cooking. Shake collander to remove excess water.

Place in closed plastic bag and refrigerate until cold, about 1 hour or overnight.

When chilled, place ½ cup noodles on each of 10 dessert plates. Top each mound of noodles with ⅓ cup yogurt and 2 tablespoons raspberries.

Nutritional Data

PER SERVING		EXCHANGES	
Calories:	170	Milk:	1.0
% Calories from fat:	10	Veg.:	0.0
Fat (gm):	2	Fruit:	0.0
Sat. fat (gm):	0.3	Bread:	1.0
Cholesterol (mg):	2	Meat:	0.0
Sodium (mg):	65	Fat:	0.5
Protein (gm):	7		
Carbohydrate (gm):	32		

CHOCOLATE NOODLES WITH APPLES AND CINNAMON

This upscale comfort food is good either hot or cold.

6 Servings, each ½ cup

Non-stick cooking spray
2 qts. water
½ recipe Chocolate Fettuccine Noodles (preceding)
3 tablespoons diet margarine, divided
2 tablespoons fructose (fruit sugar, see p. 3)
1 teaspoon cinnamon plus a few pinches for sprinkling on top
1 cup coarsely chopped peeled apples

Adjust oven rack to center position. Heat oven to 350 degrees. Spray 4-cup ovenproof casserole with non-stick spray.

Heat water to boil. Cook noodles 5 minutes or until tender. Drain in collander and run cold water over to stop cooking.

Melt 2 tablespoons margarine in large frying pan and stir in fructose and cinnamon. Stir in chopped apples and mix well. Toss with noodles.

Place noodle mixture in prepared casserole. Dot with remaining margarine and sprinkle with few pinches cinnamon.

Bake 30 minutes. Remove from oven and serve immediately from casserole.

Nutritional Data

PER SERVING		EXCHANGES	
Calories:	134	Milk:	0.0
% Calories from fat:	29	Veg.:	0.0
Fat (gm):	4	Fruit:	0.5
Sat. fat (gm):	0.7	Bread:	1.0
Cholesterol (mg):	0	Meat:	0.0
Sodium (mg):	81	Fat:	0.5
Protein (gm):	3		
Carbohydrate (gm):	22		

6.
BREADS AND MUFFINS

Southern Spoon Bread
Cocoa Banana Bread
Carob (Chocolate) Raisin Whole-Wheat Bread
Cocoa Zucchini Muffins
Cocoa Bran Muffins
Chocolate French Toast with Strawberry Sauce
Cocoa Skillet Souffle

SOUTHERN SPOON BREAD

Dried cherries and cocoa transform the spoon bread into a souffle-like dessert. Eat it with a spoon or fork.

8 Servings
Butter-flavored, non-stick cooking spray
2 cups skim milk
½ cup white cornmeal
3 tablespoons unsweetened Dutch cocoa
½ teaspoon fructose (fruit sugar, see p. 3)
½ teaspoon baking powder
¼ teaspoon salt
6 tablespoons real egg substitute
3½ tablespoons diet margarine, melted
3 egg whites, beaten
⅓ cup dried cherries (optional)

Preheat oven to 350 degrees. Spray 2-quart baking dish or casserole. Using medium saucepan, scald milk over medium-low heat. Whisk in cornmeal and cocoa. Continue cooking until mixture thickens. Remove pan from heat; cool.

Mix in fructose, baking powder, salt, egg substitute, and margarine. Fold in firmly beaten egg whites.

Spoon batter into prepared dish. Bake 30 to 40 minutes. Spoon bread will be golden and puffy. Rush to table and serve hot. Spoon onto individual dishes and top with cherries, if desired.

Nutritional Data

PER SERVING		EXCHANGES	
Calories:	91	Milk:	0.0
% Calories from fat:	28	Veg.:	0.0
Fat (gm):	3	Fruit:	0.0
Sat. fat (gm):	0.6	Bread:	1.0
Cholesterol (mg):	1	Meat:	0.0
Sodium (mg):	213	Fat:	0.5
Protein (gm):	5		
Carbohydrate (gm):	11		

COCOA BANANA BREAD

Kelley was here for the Banana Bread testing. He said, "Wonderful, a slight hint of banana and a slight taste of chocolate and so moist." The cocoa adds a chocolate taste to this already sweet shortbread. One of our children always thought this batter was good enough to eat raw. Stores well, if wrapped well.

12 Servings, 1 slice each

Butter-flavored, non-stick cooking spray
- ¼ cup diet margarine
- ¾ cup fructose (fruit sugar, see p. 3)
- 2 medium-ripe bananas, mashed
- 2 egg whites
- 1¾ cups all-purpose flour
- 3 tablespoons unsweetened Dutch cocoa
- ¼ teaspoon salt
- 1 teaspoon each ingredient: baking soda, baking powder
- ½ cup non-fat vanilla yogurt
- 1 teaspoon vanilla

Preheat oven to 350 degrees. Spray loaf pan and dust lightly with flour. Set aside.

In large bowl of electric mixer, beat margarine and fructose. Mix in mashed bananas and egg whites. Add flour, cocoa, salt, baking soda, and baking powder. Add yogurt and vanilla. Batter should be smooth.

Pour batter into prepared pan. Bake in center of oven 50 to 60 minutes. Cake will test done when tester or bamboo skewer inserted in cake comes out dry.

Let stand 5 minutes. Unmold and cool on wire rack. Slice and serve.

Nutritional Data

PER SERVING		EXCHANGES	
Calories:	168	Milk:	0.0
% Calories from fat:	22	Veg.:	0.0
Fat (gm):	4	Fruit:	1.0
Sat. fat (gm):	0.8	Bread:	1.0
Cholesterol (mg):	0.2	Meat:	0.0
Sodium (mg):	200	Fat:	1.0
Protein (gm):	3		
Carbohydrate (gm):	30		

CAROB (CHOCOLATE) RAISIN WHOLE-WHEAT BREAD

Carob adds an interesting flavor to a bread. This recipe could even be served for dessert with non-cholesterol yogurt or cream cheese. Add dried cherries for an extra treat. Try it for French toast or regular toast for breakfast.

16 Servings, 1 slice each

3–3¼ cups all-purpose flour
 1 cup whole-wheat flour
 3 tablespoons carob powder, or unsweetened Dutch cocoa
 1 cup skim milk
 ¼ cup diet margarine
 2 teaspoons fructose (fruit sugar, see p. 3)
 1 pkg. fast-rise active yeast
 1 tablespoon skim milk
 ½ cup raisins
   Butter-flavored, non-stick cooking spray
 1 tablespoon sugar

I n large mixing bowl, sift flours and carob (or cocoa) together. Set aside.

Scald milk with margarine. Cool milk slightly. Stir in fructose and yeast.

Stir milk into flour; you can use an electric mixer fitted with dough hook. Knead about 3 minutes. Dough will be soft and slightly sticky. Knead 1 minute longer on floured board. Add more flour if necessary. Dough should be soft.

Put dough in bowl, cover lightly, and set in warm, draft-free area to double in size in about 45 minutes. Punch dough down; turn it out on lightly floured board, and knead about 2 minutes. Mix in raisins.

Spray a loaf pan. Shape dough to fit pan. Brush dough with milk and sugar.

Cover and allow dough to double in size.

Preheat oven to 375 degrees. Bake bread in center of oven about 35 minutes. Bread is done when it makes a hollow sound when tapped. Cool on wire rack.

Nutritional Data

PER SERVING		EXCHANGES	
Calories:	152	Milk:	0.0
% Calories from fat:	11	Veg.:	0.0
Fat (gm):	2	Fruit:	1.0
Sat. fat (gm):	0.3	Bread:	1.5
Cholesterol (mg):	0.3	Meat:	0.0
Sodium (mg):	43	Fat:	0.0
Protein (gm):	4		
Carbohydrate (gm):	31		

Cocoa Zucchini Muffins

To make cocoa zucchini bread instead of muffins, prepare the batter in the same way, but bake it in a sprayed loaf pan about 50 minutes or until it tests done. After cooling, sprinkle on confectioners' sugar, if desired.

12 Servings, 1 muffin each

1¾ cups all-purpose flour
¼ cup cocoa
1 teaspoon each ingredient: baking powder, baking soda
¼ teaspoon salt
½ cup real egg substitute
½ cup fructose (fruit sugar, see p. 3)
2 tablespoons diet margarine, room temperature
¾ cup unpeeled, grated zucchini
⅓ cup plain non-fat yogurt

P reheat oven to 400 degrees. Set paper liners in cupcake pan.

In deep mixing bowl, blend flour, cocoa, baking powder, baking soda, and salt.

Stir in egg substitute, fructose, margarine, and zucchini. Do not over mix. Blend in yogurt.

Spoon muffin batter into paper liners.

Bake muffins in center of oven 20 to 25 minutes. Muffins are done when cake tester inserted in center comes out dry. Cool on wire rack. Serve warm.

Nutritional Data

PER SERVING		EXCHANGES	
Calories:	112	Milk:	0.0
% Calories from fat:	10	Veg.:	0.0
Fat (gm):	1	Fruit:	0.5
Sat. fat (gm):	0.2	Bread:	1.0
Cholesterol (mg):	0.1	Meat:	0.0
Sodium (mg):	182	Fat:	0.0
Protein (gm):	4		
Carbohydrate (gm):	22		

COCOA BRAN MUFFINS

Cocoa adds character to traditional bran muffins. Cool, cover, and freeze muffins for later use. Also, you can add dried cranberries, cherries, or raisins to the batter, if desired.

---

12 Servings, 1 muffin each

1½   cups bran cereal
1¼   cups skim milk
2   egg whites, slightly beaten
2   tablespoons diet margarine, melted, cooled
1¼   cups all-purpose flour
3   tablespoons cocoa
⅓   cup fructose (fruit sugar, see p. 3)
¼   teaspoon salt
1   tablespoon each ingredient: baking soda, grated orange peel

Preheat oven to 400 degrees. Set paper liners in cupcake pan.
   Using a mixing bowl, blend cereal with milk. Stir in beaten egg whites and margarine. Blend in flour, cocoa, fructose, salt, baking soda, and grated orange peel.
   Spoon batter into prepared pan. Bake 17 to 20 minutes or until muffins are golden brown and cake tester or bamboo skewer comes out dry.
   Cool out of pan. Serve warm or cold.

Nutritional Data

PER SERVING		EXCHANGES	
Calories:	109	Milk:	0.0
% Calories from fat:	13	Veg.:	0.0
Fat (gm):	2	Fruit:	0.5
Sat. fat (gm):	0.3	Bread:	1.0
Cholesterol (mg):	0.4	Meat:	0.0
Sodium (mg):	352	Fat:	0.0
Protein (gm):	4		
Carbohydrate (gm):	22		

CHOCOLATE FRENCH TOAST WITH STRAWBERRY SAUCE

You can vary the type of bread to suit your individual taste. Serve with light maple syrup, if desired. The bitter seeds of the tropical cacao tree are the source of chocolate. The Aztecs made a drink from these ground beans and water and were perhaps the first chocoholics.

4 Servings

- 1 cup real egg substitute
- 1 cup skim milk
- 2 tablespoons unsweetened Dutch cocoa
- 1 tablespoon fructose (fruit sugar, see p. 3)
- 1½ tablespoons diet margarine
- 4 slices non-cholesterol white bread or French bread
- **Strawberry Sauce** (recipe follows)

In soup bowl or other large, shallow bowl, blend egg substitute, milk, cocoa, and fructose.

Melt margarine in non-stick frying pan over medium heat.

Dip each slice of bread in chocolate milk mixture on both sides. Cook until toast is lightly browned on both sides, 2 to 3 minutes on each side.

Serve toast hot with Strawberry Sauce.

Strawberry Sauce

- 2 cups sliced strawberries
- ½ cup water
- 2 tablespoons cornstarch
- ¼ cup orange juice
- 2 teaspoons aspartame

To prepare sauce, cook strawberries with water in small saucepan over medium heat about 3 minutes, stirring often. Mix cornstarch with orange juice and whisk into sauce. Continue cooking until sauce thickens slightly. Remove from heat; cool. Stir in aspartame. Taste to adjust sweetness. Pour into sauce bowl; serve warm or cool.

Nutritional Data

PER SERVING		EXCHANGES	
Calories:	212	Milk:	0.0
% Calories from fat:	16	Veg.:	0.0
Fat (gm):	4	Fruit:	1.5
Sat. fat (gm):	0.7	Bread:	1.0
Cholesterol (mg):	1	Meat:	1.0
Sodium (mg):	284	Fat:	0.6
Protein (gm):	11		
Carbohydrate (gm):	34		

COCOA SKILLET SOUFFLE

This not-too-sweet souffle makes a wonderful brunch or late-evening snack.

2 Servings

3 tablespoons unsweetened Dutch cocoa
7 tablespoons evaporated skim milk, divided
4 tablespoons fructose (fruit sugar, see p. 3), divided
¼ cup real egg substitute
2 large egg whites
¼ teaspoon cream of tartar
  Non-stick cooking spray

P lace cocoa in small bowl and add 4 tablespoons milk. Whisk until smooth. Add remaining 3 tablespoons milk and 2 tablespoons fructose and mix well. You will have ⅔ cup mixture.

Measure out ⅓ cup mixture, pour into small saucepan, and reserve; this will be heated later for sauce.

Combine remaining ⅓ cup cocoa mixture with egg substitute, mixing well.

Beat egg whites until they hold soft peaks; add cream of tartar and continue beating until stiff. With beaters running, add remaining 2 tablespoons fructose in steady stream; turn off beaters as soon as sugar is incorporated. Fold meringue into cocoa/egg mixture.

Meanwhile, spray and heat 10-inch-diameter frying pan (measured rim to rim). Spoon mixture into pan and cook 10 minutes over low heat.

Note: Since chocolate burns easily, watch carefully to see that bottom of souffle does not burn.

As soon as bottom is set (top will still be fluffy-soft), ease omelet onto serving platter. Heat reserved sauce and pour around sides of omelet. Cut in half to serve.

Nutritional Data

PER SERVING		EXCHANGES	
Calories:	161	Milk:	0.5
% Calories from fat:	5	Veg.:	0.0
Fat (gm):	0.9	Fruit:	1.0
Sat. fat (gm):	0.3	Bread:	0.0
Cholesterol (mg):	2	Meat:	1.0
Sodium (mg):	165	Fat:	0.0
Protein (gm):	12		
Carbohydrate (gm):	30		

7.

GELATINS AND FRUITS

Chocolate Charlotte Russe

Chocolate Molded Rice with Cherries

Coffee Molded Rice

Coffee Sour Cream Mold

Apple Casserole with Chocolate Streusel

Chocolate Apple Toss

Cocoa Pineapple Whip

Wine-Poached Pears with Chocolate Sauce

Chocolate Yogurt with Berries

Chocolate "Jelly"

CHOCOLATE CHARLOTTE RUSSE

This good-tasting, old-fashioned dessert can be made with either fructose sugar or 3½ teaspoons aspartame sweetener. If you use aspartame, stir it in with the vanilla.

12 Servings

18–24	packaged lady fingers
¼	cup unsweetened Dutch cocoa
3	cups skim milk, divided
½	cup fructose (fruit sugar, see p. 3) (or 3½ teaspoons aspartame)
2	tablespoons unflavored gelatin
¼	cup cold water
1½	teaspoons vanilla
2	envelopes whipped topping mix
	Confectioners' sugar

Line bottom and sides of shallow, 8-cup, flat-bottomed casserole with split lady fingers, curved sides toward perimeter of bowl.

Place cocoa in saucepan along with ⅓ cup skim milk. Whisk until smooth. Add fructose and 1⅔ cups additional skim milk. Heat, stirring, for a few moments until mixture is smooth and warm.

Place gelatin in top of double-boiler and sprinkle with cold water to soften. Melt gelatin over simmering water. Stir gelatin into warm cocoa mixture. Allow to cool slightly, then stir in vanilla. Cover and refrigerate.

When mixture begins to set and is consistency of thick egg whites, empty 2 envelopes whipped topping mix into large bowl of electric mixer. Add 1 cup skim milk and mix with wire whisk until well combined.

Beat according to package directions until topping holds stiff peaks. Fold into cocoa/gelatin mixture.

Spoon mixture carefully over lady fingers. Cover and refrigerate until set.

At serving time, invert onto serving platter. Sprinkle with confectioners' sugar. Cut into quarters; then cut each quarter into 3 pieces.

Nutritional Data

PER SERVING		EXCHANGES	
Calories:	140	Milk:	0.0
% Calories from fat:	12	Veg.:	0.0
Fat (gm):	2	Fruit:	0.0
Sat. fat (gm):	0.6	Bread:	2.0
Cholesterol (mg):	61	Meat:	0.0
Sodium (mg):	66	Fat:	0.0
Protein (gm):	6		
Carbohydrate (gm):	24		

CHOCOLATE MOLDED RICE WITH CHERRIES

This beautiful French specialty, famous throughout Europe, is known in France as Chocolat Riz à l'Imperatrice and in Germany as Reis Trautmannsdorff. Since it makes a large mold, it's perfect for a buffet.
The dish is classically made with whole milk, whipped cream, and candied cherries. Our chocolate version, however, is delicious and much healthier with its skim milk, whipped topping mix, and non-candied cherries.

28 Servings, ½ cup each

  3 cans (16–17 ozs. each) dark sweet cherries, syrup packed
     Skim milk:
     A) enough to measure 3½ cups liquid when combined with cherry syrup from 3 cans
     B) ½ cup to combine with cocoa
     C) 1½ cups to use in whipped topping mix
1¼ cups long-grain rice (do not use quick cooking)
  5 tablespoons unsweetened Dutch cocoa
  ¾ cup fructose (fruit sugar, see p. 3)
  1 teaspoon vanilla extract
  3 envelopes unflavored gelatin
  ½ cup cold water
  3 envelopes whipped topping mix

Drain cherries from 3 cans. Reserve cherries and measure liquid. Add enough milk to cherry syrup to equal 3½ cups liquid. Combine with rice in heavy-bottomed saucepan.

Heat to boil over medium heat, reduce heat to low, and cover. Cook rice about 20 minutes or until soft but not mushy. Let rice cool a few minutes in own liquid; do not strain.

Meanwhile, combine cocoa with ½ cup skim milk; stir with wire whisk until smooth. Stir into cooked rice mixture. Then stir in fructose and vanilla.

Place gelatin in top of double-boiler. Sprinkle water over gelatin to soften. Melt gelatin over simmering water until completely dissolved. Add to cocoa/rice mixture, mixing well.

Transfer rice mixture to large bowl, cover, and refrigerate until it just begins to set up.

When mixture is partly set, place whipped topping mix in large bowl of electric mixer. Add 1½ cups skim milk and stir with whisk to combine.

Beat according to package directions until mixture holds stiff peaks. Fold whipped topping mixture into rice mixture. Then fold in cherries.

Spoon into 12- or 14-cup ring mold (or any desired mold) and pack lightly with wooden spoon. If using 12-cup ring mold, don't worry if mixture is slightly higher than sides.

Cover and refrigerate overnight or until completely set.

To unmold, dip mold in warm water. Carefully run a small knife around rim. Invert onto serving platter.

Nutritional Data

PER SERVING		EXCHANGES	
Calories:	99	Milk:	0.0
% Calories from fat:	2	Veg.:	0.0
Fat (gm):	0.2	Fruit:	1.0
Sat. fat (gm):	0.1	Bread:	0.5
Cholesterol (mg):	0.5	Meat:	0.0
Sodium (mg):	47	Fat:	0.0
Protein (gm):	2		
Carbohydrate (gm):	21		

COFFEE MOLDED RICE

◆

Molded rice should be prepared the day before serving. For a variation, omit the coffee and liqueur and add 1 cup (no-sugar added) chopped apricots.

8 Servings

- 2 cups skim milk
- 1 packet sugar-free hot cocoa mix
- 1½ teaspoons instant coffee (espresso if available)
- 1 tablespoon coffee liqueur
- 1 cup cooked rice
- ⅓ cup fructose (fruit sugar, see p. 3)
- 2 packets unflavored gelatin
- ¼ cup water

  Butter-flavored, non-stick cooking spray

Whisk milk, cocoa mix, and instant coffee into heavy saucepan; scald, stirring often. Cool. Add liqueur. Pour into deep mixing bowl. Stir in rice and fructose.

In small cup, sprinkle gelatin over water; stir and soften about 5 minutes. Pour into small saucepan and simmer, stirring often, until melted. Stir gelatin into rice mixture.

Refrigerate until just beginning to set.

Spray a 6-cup mold. Spoor or pour rice mixture into mold. Cover with sprayed waxed paper. Chill overnight.

When ready to serve, remove paper and run knife around inside of mold to loosen it. Invert mold onto serving dish.

Nutritional Data

PER SERVING		EXCHANGES	
Calories:	100	Milk:	0.5
% Calories from fat:	2	Veg.:	0.0
Fat (gm):	0.2	Fruit:	0.5
Sat. fat (gm):	0.1	Bread:	0.5
Cholesterol (mg):	1	Meat:	0.0
Sodium (mg):	63	Fat:	0.0
Protein (gm):	5		
Carbohydrate (gm):	18		

COFFEE
SOUR CREAM MOLD

Rich as the name sounds, the no-calorie sour cream now on the market allows us to have the delicious taste and texture of sour cream with none of the fat.

10 Servings, ¹/₂ cup each

1 tablespoon plus ½ teaspoon unflavored gelatin
¼ cup cold water
2 tablespoons unsweetened Dutch cocoa
8 tablespoons fructose (fruit sugar, see p. 3), divided
¼ cup skim milk
2 cups no-fat sour cream
1 teaspoon vanilla
2 egg whites
¼ teaspoon cream of tartar

Place gelatin in top of double-boiler and sprinkle with cold water to soften. Melt over simmering water.

Place cocoa and 6 tablespoons fructose in top of double-boiler and add skim milk. Stir with wire whisk until smooth. Mix in sour cream and heat over simmering water, stirring constantly, until just warm.

Add gelatin, mixing well; then stir in vanilla.

Cover and refrigerate until consistency of unbeaten egg whites.

Beat egg whites until they hold soft peaks. Add cream of tartar and beat until they hold stiff peaks. With beaters running, add remaining 2 tablespoons fructose in thin stream. Shut off beaters when fructose has been incorporated.

Fold meringue into cocoa/sour cream mixture. Spoon into 6-cup mold or glass serving bowl. Cover and refrigerate until serving time.

At serving time, bring bowl to table. Or if you've put mixture into mold, dip mold in warm water, then invert onto serving platter.

Nutritional Data

PER SERVING		EXCHANGES	
Calories:	65	Milk:	0.0
% Calories from fat:	1	Veg.:	0.0
Fat (gm):	0.1	Fruit:	0.0
Sat. fat (gm):	trace	Bread:	0.5
Cholesterol (mg):	0.1	Meat:	0.5
Sodium (mg):	39	Fat:	0.0
Protein (gm):	7		
Carbohydrate (gm):	10		

APPLE CASSEROLE WITH CHOCOLATE STREUSEL

Judging by this recipe, chocolate and apples have as much affinity as chocolate and oranges or chocolate and coffee.

6 Servings

Chocolate Streusel
Non-stick cooking spray
6 tablespoons fructose (fruit sugar, see p. 3)
6 tablespoons flour
1 tablespoon unsweetened Dutch cocoa
1 teaspoon cinnamon
3 tablespoons diet margarine

Apple Layer
6 sweet apples, peeled, cored, and cut into thick slices
2 tablespoons fructose
Cinnamon, several large pinches

Heat oven to 350 degrees and place rack in center. Spray a 10 x 8-inch shallow ovenproof casserole or a 9 x 9-inch baking pan with non-stick spray.

Streusel: Combine fructose, flour, cocoa, and cinnamon in bowl. Add margarine and use fingertips to lightly knead all ingredients together until mixture forms large clumps. Refrigerate streusel.

Apple Layer: Place half of apple slices on bottom of casserole. Sprinkle with 1 tablespoon fructose. Sprinkle several large pinches of cinnamon over apples. Add remaining apple slices to casserole and sprinkle with remaining fructose and cinnamon. Bake 30 minutes and remove from oven.

Strew Streusel over apple casserole. Return to oven for 10 minutes. Serve immediately.

Nutritional Data

PER SERVING		EXCHANGES	
Calories:	177	Milk:	0.0
% Calories from fat:	17	Veg.:	0.0
Fat (gm):	3	Fruit:	2.5
Sat. fat (gm):	0.6	Bread:	0.0
Cholesterol (mg):	0	Meat:	0.0
Sodium (mg):	66	Fat:	0.5
Protein (gm):	1		
Carbohydrate (gm):	38		

CHOCOLATE APPLE TOSS

A great dish for the fall when apples are plentiful.

8 Servings

Butter-flavored, non-stick cooking spray
½ cup all-purpose flour
2 teaspoons baking powder
¼ cup real egg substitute
1 tablespoon diet margarine
1 tablespoon unsweetened cocoa
1 teaspoon vanilla
¾ cup golden raisins
4 cups cooking apples, peeled and diced
¾ cup raspberries, optional

Preheat oven to 400 degrees. Spray an 8 x 8 x 2-inch baking pan. In large mixing bowl, toss all ingredients. Spoon mixture into prepared pan. Bake in center of oven 35 minutes. It will form a light, firm crust, and apples will be tender.

Spoon into sauce dishes and serve warm.

Nutritional Data

PER SERVING		EXCHANGES	
Calories:	120	Milk:	0.0
% Calories from fat:	8	Veg.:	0.0
Fat (gm):	1.1	Fruit:	1.5
Sat. fat (gm):	0.2	Bread:	0.5
Cholesterol (mg):	0	Meat:	0.0
Sodium (mg):	110	Fat:	0.0
Protein (gm):	2		
Carbohydrate (gm):	27		

COCOA PINEAPPLE WHIP

You can make this treat the day before and keep it chilled until served.

6 Servings

1 pkg. unflavored gelatin
1 cup water, divided
⅔ cup fructose (fruit sugar, see p. 3)
2 tablespoons unsweetened cocoa
½ teaspoon chocolate extract
½ teaspoon vanilla
2 cups unsweetened crushed pineapple, drained

S often gelatin by sprinkling it over ½ cup cold water; stir and let stand 3 to 5 minutes.

In small saucepan, heat remaining ½ cup water and stir in gelatin. Stir while gelatin melts. Pour into bowl. Stir in fructose, cocoa, chocolate extract, vanilla, and pineapple.

Refrigerate until whip begins to set.

Beat mixture with electric mixer. Pour into 6 footed glasses. Refrigerate until set and serve chilled.

Nutritional Data

PER SERVING		EXCHANGES	
Calories:	98	Milk:	0.0
% Calories from fat:	2	Veg.:	0.0
Fat (gm):	0.2	Fruit:	1.5
Sat. fat (gm):	trace	Bread:	0.0
Cholesterol (mg):	0	Meat:	0.0
Sodium (mg):	3	Fat:	0.0
Protein (gm):	2		
Carbohydrate (gm):	24		

Wine-Poached Pears with Chocolate Sauce

Chocolate sauce is good with other fruits also. For example, try it with sliced bananas or peaches.

6 Servings

2 cups dry white wine
2 cups water, or enough to cover pears
3 tablespoons lemon juice, freshly squeezed
⅓ cup fructose (fruit sugar, see p. 3)
6 firm ripe pears, peeled, cored; leave stems intact
Chocolate Sauce (recipe follows)

In medium saucepan, combine wine, water, lemon juice, and fructose. Bring poaching liquid to boil over medium heat. Reduce heat to simmer; cover. Continue simmering 10 minutes.

While liquid is heating, prepare pears. Slide pears into poaching liquid. Continue cooking 6 to 8 minutes or until pears are tender but not mushy. Cool pears in liquid.

Chocolate Sauce

Makes ¾ cup

3 tablespoons cocoa
1 tablespoon cornstarch
½ cup plus 2 tablespoons water
1 teaspoon vanilla
½ teaspoon chocolate extract
2 teaspoons aspartame, or to taste

To prepare sauce, whisk together cocoa, cornstarch, water, vanilla, and chocolate extract in small, heavy saucepan. Cook until mixture comes to boil, whisking almost constantly. Continue cooking 1 minute. Cool and mix in aspartame.

Remove pears with slotted spoon. Place each pear in shallow dish and drizzle with Chocolate Sauce.

Nutritional Data

PER SERVING		EXCHANGES	
Calories:	203	Milk:	0.0
% Calories from fat:	4	Veg.:	0.0
Fat (gm):	1	Fruit:	2.0
Sat. fat (gm):	0.2	Bread:	1.0
Cholesterol (mg):	0.7	Meat:	0.0
Sodium (mg):	113	Fat:	0.0
Protein (gm):	3		
Carbohydrate (gm):	46		

CHOCOLATE YOGURT WITH BERRIES

Every good cook stocks their personal recipe file with some very easy and elegant choices. Try this recipe with blackberries or drained mandarin orange segments. It is sure to please any sweet tooth.

4 Servings

- 2 cups non-fat vanilla yogurt
- 2 tablespoons unsweetened cocoa
- 2 teaspoons fructose (fruit sugar, see p. 3)
- ½ pt. fresh or frozen (defrosted) raspberries
- ½ pt. fresh strawberries, hulled and sliced.

 Spoon yogurt into bowl. Mix in cocoa and fructose. Divide cocoa/yogurt mixture into 4 stemmed glasses. Top with berries.

Nutritional Data

PER SERVING		EXCHANGES	
Calories:	128	Milk:	1.0
% Calories from fat:	4	Veg.:	0.0
Fat (gm):	0.6	Fruit:	1.0
Sat. fat (gm):	0.1	Bread:	0.0
Cholesterol (mg):	2	Meat:	0.0
Sodium (mg):	72	Fat:	0.0
Protein (gm):	7		
Carbohydrate (gm):	27		

CHOCOLATE "JELLY"

◆

Like all gelatin dishes, care must be taken that the no-fat sour cream is at room temperature when added to the gelatin or the gelatin will form clumps. If desired, serve jelly with whipped topping mix. Use 1 envelope whipped topping mix and ½ cup cold skim milk, and make it according to manufacturer's directions.

◆

6 Servings, ⅔ cup each

2 envelopes plus ½ teaspoon unflavored gelatin
½ cup water
6 tablespoons unsweetened Dutch cocoa
3 cups skim milk, divided
1 cup no-fat sour cream
2 teaspoons aspartame
½ teaspoon vanilla

Place gelatin in top of double-boiler and add ½ cup water. Heat until gelatin is melted. Set aside.

Place cocoa in bowl and add ½ cup milk. Stir with wire whisk until cocoa paste is smooth.

In saucepan, heat remaining 2½ cups milk until just warm, not hot. Remove from heat and add cocoa mixture to remaining milk; mix well with whisk. Add sour cream and whisk again until very well mixed. Mixture should still be warm.

Stir in aspartame and vanilla. Finally, stir in melted gelatin, mixing well. Spoon mixture into 4-cup mold. Refrigerate, covered, until set.

At serving time, dip mold in pan of warm water for a few seconds and shake lightly to loosen sides. Invert mold onto serving platter. Serve with whipped topping, if desired.

Nutritional Data

PER SERVING		EXCHANGES	
Calories:	116	Milk:	1.0
% Calories from fat:	6	Veg.:	0.0
Fat (gm):	0.8	Fruit:	0.5
Sat. fat (gm):	0.3	Bread:	0.0
Cholesterol (mg):	2	Meat:	0.0
Sodium (mg):	80	Fat:	0.0
Protein (gm):	11		
Carbohydrate (gm):	17		

8.
COOKIES

Brownies
♦
Carob Shell Cookies
♦
Cocoa Peanut Butter Cookies
♦
Cocoa Meringue Cookies
♦
Cocoa Raisin Cookies
♦
Cocoa Gingerbread Star Cookies
♦
Cocoa Sponge Drops

BROWNIES

These brownies taste better cold. They are surprisingly low in fat but rich in flavor and easy to make.

12 Servings, 1 brownie each

Butter-flavored, non-stick cooking spray
- ¼ cup real egg substitute
- ¼ cup diet margarine, melted, cooled
- ¾ cup fructose (fruit sugar, see p. 3)
- 2 tablespoons water
- 3 tablespoons cocoa
- 2¾ cups fine, plain breadcrumbs
- ¼ teaspoon salt
- ½ teaspoon baking powder
- ½ cup golden raisins

Preheat oven to 350 degrees. Spray a 9 x 8-inch-square baking pan. In bowl of electric mixer, mix egg substitute, cooled margarine, and fructose.

In separate bowl, mix water and cocoa together; it will be stiff. Add to batter. Blend in crumbs, salt, baking powder, and raisins.

Pour batter into prepared pan. Bake in center of oven 25 to 30 minutes. When done, a cake tester will come out dry, and top of brownies will be firm to the touch.

Cool. Cut into 12 squares.

Nutritional Data

PER SERVING		EXCHANGES	
Calories:	168	Milk:	0.0
% Calories from fat:	17	Veg.:	0.0
Fat (gm):	3	Fruit:	1.0
Sat. fat (gm):	0.6	Bread:	1.0
Cholesterol (mg):	0	Meat:	0.0
Sodium (mg):	278	Fat:	0.5
Protein (gm):	4		
Carbohydrate (gm):	32		

CAROB SHELL COOKIES

Use a Madeleine, or shell, pan (available at gourmet food shops) to bake these pretty, shell-shaped, sponge-textured cookies. Add a sprinkle of confectioners' sugar before serving.

19 Servings, 2 cookies each

Butter-flavored, non-stick cooking spray

1¼ cups all-purpose flour

½ teaspoon baking powder

3 tablespoons carob powder, or cocoa

1½ cups real egg substitute

½ cup fructose (fruit sugar, see p. 3)

½ cup diet margarine, melted, cooled

1 tablespoon cornstarch

2 egg whites, beaten stiff

Spray a Madeleine pan. Preheat oven to 375 degrees.

Into mixing bowl, sift flour, baking powder, and carob powder.

With whisk or electric mixer, beat together egg substitute and fructose until combined. Stir in cooled margarine. Fold in flour mixture, cornstarch, and egg whites.

Spoon batter, ¾ full, into depressions in pan. Bake in center of oven 12 to 15 minutes. When done, cookies will be firm and spring back when touched.

Cool about 5 minutes in pan. Turn out cookies. Some may require loosening with small knife. Cool completely before serving.

Nutritional Data

PER SERVING		EXCHANGES	
Calories:	82	Milk:	0.0
% Calories from fat:	27	Veg.:	0.0
Fat (gm):	2	Fruit:	0.0
Sat. fat (gm):	0.4	Bread:	1.0
Cholesterol (mg):	0	Meat:	0.0
Sodium (mg):	96	Fat:	0.0
Protein (gm):	2		
Carbohydrate (gm):	12		

Cocoa Peanut Butter Cookies

If dough is too soft to handle, refrigerate it first for 1 hour.

22 Servings, 1 cookie each

1½ cups all-purpose flour
3 tablespoons unsweetened Dutch cocoa
1½ teaspoons baking powder
½ teaspoon salt
¼ cup diet margarine, room temperature
½ cup chunky peanut butter
1½ teaspoons vanilla
¼ cup real egg substitute
⅓ cup orange juice
⅓ cup fructose (fruit sugar, see p. 3)
¾ cup dark raisins

Preheat oven to 400 degrees. Sift together flour, cocoa, baking powder, and salt.

In electric mixer bowl, cream margarine, peanut butter, and vanilla. Stir in egg substitute, orange juice, and fructose. Blend in flour mixture and raisins. Dough will be soft. Flour hands lightly before rolling cookies into balls.

Roll 1 tablespoon dough between hands, to form balls. Set cookies 1½ inches apart on ungreased, non-stick cookie sheet. Flatten cookies using fork.

Bake 12 to 15 minutes. Cookies will begin to brown on bottom and turn a light golden color on top. They will be firm to the touch when done. Cool on wire rack. Store in airtight container. These cookies store well and are more flavorful the second day.

Nutritional Data

PER SERVING		EXCHANGES	
Calories:	80	Milk:	0.0
% Calories from fat:	26	Veg.:	0.0
Fat (gm):	2	Fruit:	0.0
Sat. fat (gm):	0.5	Bread:	1.0
Cholesterol (mg):	0	Meat:	0.0
Sodium (mg):	83	Fat:	0.5
Protein (gm):	2		
Carbohydrate (gm):	13		

Cocoa Meringue Cookies

It is better to bake meringues on a dry day. For most volume, use fresh eggs at room temperature.

12 Servings, 2 cookies each

- 2 egg whites, room temperature
- ½ cup, scant, sugar, divided
- 2 tablespoons unsweetened Dutch cocoa
- 1 teaspoon cream of tartar
- 1 teaspoon vanilla
- ¼ teaspoon chocolate extract

Preheat oven to 275 degrees. Line a sprayed cookie sheet with aluminum foil, parchment, or brown paper.

In electric mixer bowl, beat egg whites until soft peaks form. Sprinkle half of sugar, cocoa, and cream of tartar over whites and continue beating until incorporated. Sprinkle remaining sugar over egg whites and beat to incorporate. Add vanilla and chocolate; mix to combine.

Drop meringue, by tablespoons, onto cookie sheet.

Bake 45 minutes. Cool completely with oven door shut. Cookies should be firm to the touch.

Cover meringues and store in airtight container.

Nutritional Data

PER SERVING		EXCHANGES	
Calories:	36	Milk:	0.0
% Calories from fat:	2	Veg.:	0.0
Fat (gm):	trace	Fruit:	0.0
Sat. fat (gm):	trace	Bread:	0.0
Cholesterol (mg):	0	Meat:	0.0
Sodium (mg):	10	Fat:	0.0
Protein (gm):	0.8		
Carbohydrate (gm):	8		

COCOA RAISIN COOKIES

This is a New England-style cookie, that is, a molasses, ginger, and raisin combination. Children and grownups alike enjoy them.

24 Servings, 2 cookies each

⅔ cup golden raisins
¾ cup fructose (fruit sugar, see p. 3)
10 tablespoons diet margarine
¼ cup real egg substitute
¼ cup molasses
2 cups all-purpose flour
¼ cup cocoa
2 teaspoons baking soda
1¼ teaspoons ground cinnamon
¾ teaspoon ground ginger
¼ teaspoon each ingredient: ground allspice,
nutmeg, salt
2 tablespoons sugar

P ut raisins in small bowl. Cover with boiling water. Let stand 3 to 4 minutes; drain and set aside.

In large bowl, or electric mixer bowl, combine fructose, margarine, egg substitute, and molasses. Mix in flour, cocoa, baking soda, cinnamon, ginger, allspice, nutmeg, and salt. Mix in raisins.

Gather dough into ball; cover with plastic wrap. Chill 3 to 4 hours.

Preheat oven to 350 degrees. Break off small amounts of dough. Roll each with palms of hands into ¾-inch balls. Place sugar in shallow bowl. Roll cookies in sugar. Set cookies on ungreased, non-stick cookie sheet about 1½ inches apart.

Bake cookies about 10 minutes or until firm to touch. Cool on cookie sheet 1 to 2 minutes. Using spatula, remove cookies to rack to cool completely.

Nutritional Data

PER SERVING

Calories:	86
% Calories from fat:	4
Fat (gm):	0.4
Sat. fat (gm):	trace
Cholesterol (mg):	0
Sodium (mg):	140
Protein (gm):	1.6
Carbohydrate (gm):	20

EXCHANGES

Milk:	0.0
Veg.:	0.0
Fruit:	0.0
Bread:	1.0
Meat:	0.0
Fat:	0.0

Cocoa Gingerbread Star Cookies

◆

These cookies are good at holiday times or all year round. They are thin and spicy. You can add dried currants to the batter if desired.

15 Servings, 2 cookies each

- ½ cup dark molasses
- ¼ cup diet margarine
- 1¼ cups all-purpose flour
- 3 tablespoons unsweetened Dutch cocoa
- ¼ teaspoon baking powder
- ½ teaspoon ground ginger
- ¼ teaspoon ground nutmeg
- Butter-flavored, non-stick cooking spray

Place molasses and margarine in small saucepan over medium heat and bring to boil. Cool. Pour mixture into mixing bowl or bowl of electric mixer.

Sift together flour, cocoa, baking powder, ginger, and nutmeg. Blend into molasses mixture.

Gather dough into ball; cover with aluminum foil. Refrigerate 3 to 4 hours.

Divide dough in half. Roll it out on lightly floured board. Cut out cookies, using a "star" cutter or other pattern of your choice.

Preheat oven to 375 degrees. Spray non-stick cookie sheet. Place cookies on sheet 1½ inches apart.

Bake cookies in center of oven 8 to 10 minutes. Cookies are done when just firm and beginning to brown.

Cool in pan; remove with spatula. Store in airtight container.

Nutritional Data

PER SERVING		EXCHANGES	
Calories:	78	Milk:	0.0
% Calories from fat:	20	Veg.:	0.0
Fat (gm):	1.8	Fruit:	0.0
Sat. fat (gm):	0.4	Bread:	1.0
Cholesterol (mg):	0	Meat:	0.0
Sodium (mg):	52	Fat:	0.0
Protein (gm):	1.2		
Carbohydrate (gm):	14		

COCOA SPONGE DROPS

This chewy cookie is "frosted" with ¼ teaspoon of raspberry spread. Or stack two, using ½ teaspoon of spread.

18 Servings, 2 cookies each

Non-stick cooking spray
¼ cup real egg substitute
¼ cup fructose (fruit sugar, see p. 3)
3 tablespoons skim milk
1 teaspoon baking powder
1 teaspoon vanilla
14 tablespoons unsifted cake flour (1 cup less 2 tablespoons)
2 tablespoons unsweetened Dutch cocoa
3 tablespoons (9 teaspoons) low-sugar red raspberry spread
Confectioners' sugar

Adjust oven rack to center and preheat oven to 350 degrees. Spray cookie sheet with non-stick spray.

In electric mixer bowl, beat egg substitute with fructose, milk, baking powder, and vanilla until thick.

Sift flour with cocoa, then beat into batter, mixing well.

Drop batter, by teaspoonfuls, onto prepared cookie sheet.

Bake 10 to 12 minutes or until risen and firm when touched lightly on top.

Transfer cookies to wire rack. When cool, spread each cookie with ¼ teaspoon low-sugar red raspberry spread. Sprinkle liberally with confectioners' sugar before serving.

Nutritional Data

PER SERVING		EXCHANGES	
Calories:	18	Milk:	0.0
% Calories from fat:	3	Veg.:	0.0
Fat (gm):	0.1	Fruit:	0.0
Sat. fat (gm):	trace	Bread:	0.25
Cholesterol (mg):	trace	Meat:	0.0
Sodium (mg):	14	Fat:	0.0
Protein (gm):	0.5		
Carbohydrate (gm):	4		

9.
CHOCOLATE CHEESE

Chocolate Cheesecake
♦
Chocolate Cheese Pie
♦
Chocolate Cheesecake in a Casserole
♦
Chocolate Cheese Pizza
♦
Chocolate Cheese Ball
♦
Chocolate Crostata di Ricotta

CHOCOLATE CHEESECAKE

The use of no-fat cream cheese in this cake causes it to develop cracks on top during baking. This can be partly disguised by sprinkling confectioners' sugar lightly over it. Or, if desired, make the optional meringue (see below) to cover cake.

12 Servings

Crust
3 tablespoons diet margarine
⅔ cup graham cracker crumbs
½ teaspoon cinnamon

Filling
1 cup 1% cottage cheese, drained
¼ cup unsweetened Dutch cocoa
1¼ teaspoons vanilla extract
1 cup fructose (fruit sugar, see p. 3)
2 cups no-fat cream cheese
1 cup no-fat sour cream
½ cup real egg substitute

Meringue (optional)
1 egg white
⅛ teaspoon cream of tartar
1 tablespoon fructose

Place oven rack in center of oven and preheat oven to 350 degrees.
Crust: Melt margarine, add graham cracker crumbs and cinnamon, and mix well. Pat crust over bottom of 10-inch springform pan. Bake 5 minutes.

Filling: Place cottage cheese in food processor with cocoa and vanilla and process until smooth. Add fructose, cream cheese, and sour cream and blend again. Add egg substitute and pulse processor for a moment until well blended.

Spoon batter onto crumb crust. Bake 60 minutes.

Allow cake to cool to room temperature. Cover cake well, then refrigerate until cold.

Meringue: Heat oven to 300 degrees. Beat egg white in electric mixer bowl until it holds soft peaks. Add cream of tartar. Beat until it holds stiff peaks. With beaters running, add 1 tablespoon fructose in thin stream. Turn off beaters.

Remove sides of springform pan carefully and spread meringue over top of cake. Place in a 300-degree oven 10 or 15 minutes until meringue is golden brown.

At serving time, cut cheesecake into quarters. Cut each quarter into 3 pieces.

Nutritional Data

PER SERVING		EXCHANGES	
Calories:	161	Milk:	0.0
% Calories from fat:	13	Veg.:	0.0
Fat (gm):	2	Fruit:	1.0
Sat. fat (gm):	0.5	Bread:	0.5
Cholesterol (mg):	8	Meat:	1.0
Sodium (mg):	388	Fat:	0.0
Protein (gm):	11		
Carbohydrate (gm):	23		

CHOCOLATE CHEESE PIE

◆

The filling for this pie is made in a food processor. If you don't have one, the finished pie will taste just as good, although it will be coarser in texture. Make sure batter ingredients are at room temperature when mixed or the gelatin will form clumps when added to the batter.

10 Servings

Crust
3 tablespoons diet margarine
⅔ cup graham cracker crumbs

Filling
1½ cups 1% cottage cheese, at room temperature
⅓ cup unsweetened Dutch cocoa
1 cup no-fat cream cheese, at room temperature
Skim milk:
  ⅓ cup skim milk, at room temperature
  ½ cup cold skim milk, for whipped topping
1 tablespoon aspartame sweetener
1 teaspoon vanilla extract
½ cup water
1 envelope plus 1½ teaspoons unflavored gelatin
1 envelope whipped topping mix

Crust: Melt margarine and mix with graham crumbs. Press crumbs firmly against bottom and about ½ inch up sides of 10-inch pie pan. Bake in 375-degree oven 5 minutes; remove and allow to cool.

Filling: Place cottage cheese and cocoa in food processor or blender and blend a few seconds until smooth. Add cream cheese, ⅓ cup skim milk, aspartame, and vanilla and pulse until well mixed. If necessary, stop processor and scrape down sides of bowl.

Place ½ cup water in top of double-boiler and sprinkle gelatin over water to soften. Place double-boiler over simmering water until gelatin is melted. Use rubber spatula to scrape gelatin into cheese/cocoa batter, mixing well.

Cover batter and refrigerate until gelatin is consistency of very thick egg whites. Transfer batter to electric mixer bowl and beat for a moment. Transfer batter back to first bowl.

Place whipped topping mix in electric mixer bowl. Add remaining ½ cup milk and stir well with wire whisk.

Beat topping according to package directions until stiff. Add cheese/cocoa batter to mixer bowl. Beat a few seconds until well combined.

Spoon batter into pie pan. Lay piece of waxed paper over filling and refrigerate, covered, until set, about 4 hours.

To serve, cut pie in half, then cut each half into 5 wedges.

Nutritional Data

PER SERVING		EXCHANGES	
Calories:	133	Milk:	0.0
% Calories from fat:	22	Veg.:	0.0
Fat (gm):	3	Fruit:	0.0
Sat. fat (gm):	0.8	Bread:	1.0
Cholesterol (mg):	4	Meat:	1.0
Sodium (mg):	413	Fat:	0.0
Protein (gm):	12		
Carbohydrate (gm):	13		

CHOCOLATE CHEESECAKE IN A CASSEROLE

This cake uses 1% cottage cheese and a food processor or blender to puree it to smoothness. If you don't have the equipment, simply make a rougher textured cake using an electric mixer.

16 Servings

Crust

4½ tablespoons diet margarine
1 cup graham cracker crumbs
1 teaspoon fructose (fruit sugar, see p. 3)
1¼ teaspoons cinnamon

Filling

3 cups (1½ lbs.) 1% cottage cheese
6 tablespoons unsweetened Dutch cocoa
1 cup fructose (fruit sugar, see p. 3)
1½ teaspoons vanilla extract
¼ teaspoon chocolate extract
1 cup real egg substitute
½ cup flour
1 cup no-fat sour cream
Confectioners' sugar

Adjust oven rack to center of oven and preheat oven to 350 degrees.
Crust: Melt margarine. Combine graham cracker crumbs with 1 teaspoon fructose and cinnamon. Stir crumbs into margarine. Pat crumbs onto bottom of 9 x 13-inch glass casserole. Bake 5 minutes. Remove casserole and lower heat to 325 degrees.

Filling: Place cottage cheese in food processor with cocoa, fructose, vanilla, and chocolate extracts. Process until smooth.

Transfer to large bowl of electric mixer and combine with real egg substitute, flour, and sour cream, mixing well.

Spoon batter carefully over crumbs in casserole. Bake 75 minutes or until firm in center.

Place casserole on rack to cool. Cover and refrigerate until cold.

At serving time, cut cake into quarters. Cut each quarter into 4 pieces. Sprinkle with confectioners' sugar before serving.

Nutritional Data

PER SERVING		EXCHANGES	
Calories:	151	Milk:	0.0
% Calories from fat:	17	Veg.:	0.0
Fat (gm):	3	Fruit:	0.5
Sat. fat (gm):	0.7	Bread:	1.0
Cholesterol (mg):	2	Meat:	1.0
Sodium (mg):	280	Fat:	0.0
Protein (gm):	9		
Carbohydrate (gm):	22		

CHOCOLATE CHEESE PIZZA

The crust and filling can be prepared ahead of time and assembled at the last minute before baking the pizza.

12 Servings

Crust (12 inches)
1 cup chocolate graham cracker crumbs
2 tablespoons diet margarine, melted
½ teaspoon ground cinnamon

Filling
1 cup golden raisins
3 tablespoons dark rum
3 cups non-fat ricotta cheese
¼ cup unsweetened Dutch cocoa
1 tablespoon grated orange peel
3 tablespoons orange juice, freshly squeezed
1 tablespoon fructose (fruit sugar, see p. 3)
½ teaspoon ground cinnamon
½ cup real egg substitute
2 egg whites, beaten
¾ cup fine breadcrumbs
1 cup strawberries, washed and sliced, or raspberries

Crust: Use food processor fitted with steel blade. Combine all crust ingredients, or toss crust ingredients in bowl, using mixing spoon. Pat crumbs onto 12-inch pizza pan. Preheat oven to 375 degrees.

Filling: Soak raisins in rum 10 minutes. Spoon cheese into deep bowl. Add cocoa, raisins and rum, orange peel, orange juice, fructose, and cinnamon. Blend in egg substitute, egg whites, and crumbs. Spoon filling over crust.

Bake pizza 30 minutes. Cool, slice, and serve sprinkled with berries.

Nutritional Data

PER SERVING		EXCHANGES	
Calories:	180	Milk:	0.0
% Calories from fat:	19	Veg.:	0.0
Fat (gm):	4	Fruit:	0.0
Sat. fat (gm):	1	Bread:	1.5
Cholesterol (mg):	6	Meat:	1.0
Sodium (mg):	149	Fat:	0.5
Protein (gm):	12		
Carbohydrate (gm):	30		

CHOCOLATE CHEESE BALL

The cheese ball can be prepared days in advance. Serve it with crackers or sliced fruit, such as apples, pears, and/or clusters of grapes. Guests spread the chocolate-cheese over the slices of fruit or crackers.

8 Servings

- 8 ozs. light, non-cholesterol farmer's cheese
- ½ cup non-fat vanilla yogurt
- 2½ tablespoons unsweetened Dutch cocoa
- ½ teaspoon vanilla
- 1½ teaspoons fructose (fruit sugar, see p. 3)
- 2 teaspoons rum, coffee, or chocolate liqueur
- Cheesecloth
- Deep bowl

I n deep bowl, mix farmer's cheese and vanilla yogurt. Add cocoa, vanilla, fructose, and rum.

Cut a double thickness of cheesecloth about 1 foot square. Spoon cheese mixture into cloth, forming cheese into a ball in center of cheesecloth. Secure top of cheesecloth with knot. Suspend cheese ball on knife or chopstick over a bowl to drain. Refrigerate 24 hours.

Remove and discard cheesecloth. You may have to reshape cheese into round ball. Place on chilled serving dish with fruit or crackers.

Nutritional Data

PER SERVING		EXCHANGES	
Calories:	62	Milk:	0.5
% Calories from fat:	30	Veg.:	0.0
Fat (gm):	2	Fruit:	0.0
Sat. fat (gm):	trace	Bread:	0.0
Cholesterol (mg):	5	Meat:	0.0
Sodium (mg):	21	Fat:	0.5
Protein (gm):	4		
Carbohydrate (gm):	7		

CHOCOLATE CROSTATA DI RICOTTA

This is a healthy, chocolate version of an ancient and famous Roman dessert of the same name. It's traditionally served with fresh fruits such as pears or grapes, so add wedges or small bunches as desired. We used low-fat rather than no-fat ricotta for extra creaminess. You can substitute no-fat ricotta, if desired. If you like a strong chocolate flavor, add a little chocolate extract to taste before baking, about 1/2 teaspoon.

16 Servings

Crust

3 tablespoons diet margarine
2/3 cup graham cracker crumbs

Filling

1/2 cup unsweetened Dutch cocoa
3 tablespoons skim milk
2 teaspoons vanilla
1 cup real egg substitute, divided
5 cups low-fat ricotta cheese
1 cup fructose (fruit sugar, see p. 3)
2/3 cup candied orange peel, finely chopped

Adjust oven rack to center of oven. Preheat oven to 350 degrees.

Crust: Melt margarine and combine with graham crumbs. Pat onto bottom of 10-inch springform pan. Bake 5 minutes. Remove from oven and cool to room temperature.

Filling: Combine cocoa, skim milk, vanilla, and 1/4 cup egg substitute. Whisk with wire whisk until smooth.

Spoon ricotta cheese into bowl of electric mixer and add cocoa mixture, fructose, and remaining 3/4 cup egg substitute. Mix until well combined. Stir candied peel into batter.

Spoon batter into cooled graham cracker crust. Bake 60 minutes or until filling is set. Cool on wire rack. When cool, cover and refrigerate until chilled.

At serving time, carefully remove sides of springform. Slide bottom of springform onto serving platter. Cut torte into 16 wedges.

Nutritional Data

PER SERVING		EXCHANGES	
Calories:	158	Milk:	0.0
% Calories from fat:	20	Veg.:	0.0
Fat (gm):	4	Fruit:	0.5
Sat. fat (gm):	0.3	Bread:	1.0
Cholesterol (mg):	10	Meat:	1.0
Sodium (mg):	125	Fat:	0.0
Protein (gm):	9		
Carbohydrate (gm):	24		

10.
FROZEN CHOCOLATE

Frozen Chocolate Mousse

Chocolate Ice Milk with Bittersweet Chocolate Sauce

Cocoa Ice Milk

Orange Mocha Ice Milk

Chocolate-Spiced Freezer Pudding

Frozen Mocha Yogurt

Frozen Chocolate Mousse

This mousse looks and sounds like an Italian meringue. But it loses that definition when the cocoa is added.

8 Servings

½ cup fructose (fruit sugar, see p. 3)
1 cup water
6 large egg whites
¾ teaspoon cream of tartar
2 tablespoons unsweetened Dutch cocoa, sieved
½ teaspoon vanilla extract

C ombine fructose and water in heavy-bottomed saucepan and cook, uncovered, until candy thermometer registers 238 degrees.

Meanwhile, place egg whites in electric mixer bowl. As soon as thermometer registers 238 degrees, turn on beaters.

Beat whites until they hold soft peaks; add cream of tartar and beat until they hold stiff peaks.

When thermometer registers 238 degrees, remove pan from heat and, with beaters running, add fructose syrup to egg whites in thin stream.

When syrup has been added, turn beaters to low and add cocoa, then vanilla.

As soon as ingredients are well combined, spoon mousse into 5-cup glass serving bowl, or spoon about ½ cup into each of 9 serving dishes. Cover and freeze until firm. Serve frozen.

Nutritional Data

PER SERVING		EXCHANGES	
Calories:	52	Milk:	0.0
% Calories from fat:	2	Veg.:	0.0
Fat (gm):	0.1	Fruit:	0.5
Sat. fat (gm):	trace	Bread:	0.0
Cholesterol (mg):	0	Meat:	0.5
Sodium (mg):	42	Fat:	0.0
Protein (gm):	3		
Carbohydrate (gm):	10		

CHOCOLATE ICE MILK WITH BITTERSWEET CHOCOLATE SAUCE

After the second processing, you can freeze the ice milk in popsicle molds.

8 Servings

1 packet unflavored gelatin
2 cups skim milk
½ cup fructose (fruit sugar, see p. 3)
2 cups evaporated skim milk
¼ cup unsweetened Dutch cocoa
1 teaspoon vanilla
½ teaspoon chocolate extract
⅛ teaspoon ground nutmeg
Bittersweet Chocolate Sauce (recipe follows)

S often gelatin in 2 tablespoons cold water. Pour milk into saucepan and scald over medium heat. Remove pan from heat. Whisk in gelatin and fructose. Stir until dissolved.

Blend in evaporated milk, cocoa, vanilla, chocolate extract, and nutmeg. Pour into shallow dish.

Cover and freeze 4 hours. Break into chunks and puree, using food processor. Return to dish and refreeze until firm, 45 minutes to 1½ hours.

Spoon into dishes and serve with Bittersweet Chocolate Sauce.

Bittersweet Chocolate Sauce

1 can (10 ozs.) evaporated skim milk
¼ cup unsweetened Dutch cocoa
⅓ cup fructose (fruit sugar, see p. 3)
2 tablespoons chocolate liqueur

To make Chocolate Sauce, combine ingredients in small, heavy saucepan, and over medium heat, bring sauce to boil. Reduce heat to simmer and cook 2 to 3 minutes, stirring often. Cool. Place in covered container and chill until needed. Reheat before serving.

Nutritional Data

PER SERVING		EXCHANGES	
Calories:	175	Milk:	1.0
% Calories from fat:	4	Veg.:	0.0
Fat (gm):	0.8	Fruit:	1.5
Sat. fat (gm):	0.3	Bread:	0.0
Cholesterol (mg):	5	Meat:	0.0
Sodium (mg):	150	Fat:	0.1
Protein (gm):	11		
Carbohydrate (gm):	33		

COCOA ICE MILK

◆

This good-tasting recipe is low in fat, but still has a creamy texture due to the dry whipped topping mix, which is added toward the end of the processing. NOTE: If you don't have an ice cream maker, follow directions for Still Freezing in "Skinny Ingredients."

◆

26 Servings, ½ cup each

7 tablespoons unsweetened Dutch cocoa
7½ cups skim milk, divided
7¼ teaspoons aspartame
2 teaspoons vanilla extract
3 envelopes whipped topping mix

P lace cocoa in bowl. Add ½ cup skim milk and whisk until smooth. Add another ½ cup and whisk until well mixed.

Add another 5 cups skim milk to ice cream maker and stir in cocoa mixture with wire whisk.

Stir in aspartame and vanilla, mixing well.

Process in ice cream maker according to manufacturer's directions.

When ice milk begins to set up but is still soft, place envelopes of whipped topping mix in large bowl of electric mixer. Pour 1½ cups cold skim milk over topping and mix with wire whisk until completely combined.

Beat topping according to package directions until topping is consistency of thick whipped cream.

Turn off ice cream maker and stir topping into mixture with long-handled wooden spoon.

Continue processing until done. Transfer ice milk to large covered container and store in freezer until hardened.

Nutritional Data

PER SERVING		EXCHANGES	
Calories:	50	Milk:	0.5
% Calories from fat:	5	Veg.:	0.0
Fat (gm):	0.3	Fruit:	0.0
Sat. fat (gm):	0.1	Bread:	0.0
Cholesterol (mg):	1	Meat:	0.0
Sodium (mg):	43	Fat:	0.0
Protein (gm)·	3		
Carbohydrate (gm):	7		

ORANGE MOCHA ICE MILK

The combination of coffee, chocolate, and candied orange rind is refreshing and sophisticated. NOTE: If you don't have an ice cream maker, see directions for Still Freezing in "Skinny Ingredients."

16 Servings, 1/2 cup each

- 1 tablespoon instant coffee crystals
- 5 tablespoons unsweetened Dutch cocoa
- 6 cups skim milk, divided
- 5 teaspoons aspartame
- 4 ozs. candied orange peel
- 2 envelopes whipped topping mix

Place instant coffee crystals and cocoa in medium bowl. Add ½ cup skim milk and stir with wire whisk until smooth. Stir in an additional ½ cup skim milk, mixing well.

Place another 4 cups milk in ice cream maker, along with coffee/cocoa mixture and aspartame; stir with long-handled wooden spoon until combined.

Process in ice cream maker until mixture just begins to set up but is still soft.

Place candied peel in food processor and pulse until finely chopped.

Place dry whipped topping mix in large bowl of electric mixer, adding remaining 1 cup skim milk. Stir with wire whisk until well combined.

Beat according to package directions until mixture stands in stiff peaks.

Turn off ice cream maker. Add whipped topping to ice milk, along with chopped candied orange rind, stirring well with wooden spoon.

Continue processing until done. Transfer ice milk to covered container and store in freezer until hardened.

Nutritional Data

PER SERVING		EXCHANGES	
Calories:	82	Milk:	1.0
% Calories from fat:	4	Veg.:	0.0
Fat (gm):	0.3	Fruit:	0.0
Sat. fat (gm):	0.2	Bread:	0.0
Cholesterol (mg):	2	Meat:	0.0
Sodium (mg):	54	Fat:	0.0
Protein (gm):	4		
Carbohydrate (gm):	14		

CHOCOLATE-SPICED FREEZER PUDDING

This delicious pudding is best when frozen in a crock or casserole dish. If you freeze it in a mold, when you try to unmold it, it will get too soft.

18 Servings, ¹/₂ cup each

⅓ cup unsweetened Dutch cocoa
2 tablespoons cornstarch
⅓ cup plus 2½ cups skim milk, divided
¾ cup fructose (fruit sugar, see p. 3), divided
¼ cup real egg substitute
½ cup low-calorie strawberry jam
1 teaspoon cinnamon
Nutmeg, large pinch
Allspice, large pinch
1 envelope whipped topping mix
2 large egg whites
¼ teaspoon cream of tartar

Place cocoa, cornstarch, and ⅓ cup skim milk in small saucepan and whisk until smooth. Stir in 2 more cups skim milk and ½ cup fructose. Cook over low heat, stirring constantly, until thick.

Place egg substitute in small bowl and stir in a few spoonfuls hot cocoa mixture. Stir in a few more spoonfuls and mix again.

Add egg substitute mixture to cocoa mixture and stir well. Cook over low heat, stirring constantly, until mixture thickens.

Stir in strawberry jam, cinnamon, nutmeg, and allspice with wire whisk. Remove from heat, transfer to bowl, and allow to cool.

Cover and chill in refrigerator.

When mixture is cold, place whipped topping mix in bottom of electric mixer bowl with ½ cup milk and whisk until combined.

Beat according to package directions until thick. Fold into pudding.

Beat egg whites until they hold soft peaks; add cream of tartar and beat until they hold stiff peaks.

With beaters running, add remaining ¼ cup fructose in a thin stream. Turn off beaters as soon as sugar is incorporated.

Spoon pudding into 10-cup crock, cover, and place in freezer overnight or until firm.

At serving time, scoop out ½-cup servings.

Nutritional Data

PER SERVING		EXCHANGES	
Calories:	66	Milk:	0.5
% Calories from fat:	3	Veg.:	0.0
Fat (gm):	0.2	Fruit:	0.5
Sat. fat (gm):	0.1	Bread:	0.0
Cholesterol (mg):	0.6	Meat:	0.0
Sodium (mg):	42	Fat:	0.0
Protein (gm):	2.3		
Carbohydrate (gm):	14		

FROZEN MOCHA YOGURT

If you like coffee/chocolate flavors, you'll love this low-fat frozen dessert. NOTE: If you don't have an ice cream maker, see directions for Still Freezing in "Skinny Ingredients Primer."

12 Servings, ¹/₂ cup each

¼ cup unsweetened Dutch cocoa
1 tablespoon cornstarch
2 cans canned evaporated skim milk
2 teaspoons instant coffee crystals
1 teaspoon liquid coffee
1½ cups non-fat yogurt
7 teaspoons aspartame
2 teaspoons vanilla
3 large egg whites
¼ teaspoon cream of tartar

Combine cocoa and cornstarch in heavy-bottomed saucepan. Add ½ cup evaporated milk. Whisk until smooth with wire whisk. Stir in remaining evaporated milk. Allow to cool.

Cook over medium heat, whisking constantly, until thickened. Remove from heat and cool.

Stir coffee crystals and liquid coffee together in small bowl until dissolved.

In large bowl, blend yogurt, aspartame, and vanilla; then add mixture and coffee to cooled cocoa mixture.

Beat egg whites until they hold soft peaks; add cream of tartar and beat until they hold stiff peaks. Fold into cocoa mixture.

Transfer mixture to ice cream maker. Process in ice cream maker according to manufacturer's directions.

Transfer to covered container and store in freezer.

Nutritional Data

PER SERVING		EXCHANGES	
Calories:	64	Milk:	0.75
% Calories from fat:	4	Veg.:	0.0
Fat (gm):	0.3	Fruit:	0.0
Sat. fat (gm):	0.1	Bread:	0.0
Cholesterol (mg):	2	Meat:	0.0
Sodium (mg):	86	Fat:	0.0
Protein (gm):	6		
Carbohydrate (gm):	9		

11.
CHOCOLATE DRINKS

Creamy Mocha Cooler

Iced Mocha

Cocoa Vanilla Mix

CREAMY MOCHA COOLER

Ultra-refreshing on a hot day. Or try our creamy cocoa cooler by substituting the same amount of vanilla-flavored non-dairy creamer for the Kahlua-flavored. The calories and fat content are the same.

1 Serving of 1 cup

3   tablespoons Kahlua-flavored, fat-free, non-dairy creamer
⅓   cup cold water
2½ teaspoons unsweetened Dutch cocoa
¾   teaspoon aspartame
5   ice cubes

 Place all ingredients in blender. Blend at high speed until ice is dissolved.

Nutritional Data

PER SERVING		EXCHANGES	
Calories:	93	Milk:	0.0
% Calories from fat:	4	Veg.:	0.0
Fat (gm):	0.4	Fruit:	0.5
Sat. fat (gm):	1.0	Bread:	1.0
Cholesterol (mg):	0	Meat:	0.0
Sodium (mg):	3	Fat:	0.0
Protein (gm):	3		
Carbohydrate (gm):	20		

ICED MOCHA

◆

A particularly cooling and refreshing iced coffee/chocolate. If you don't want to use fructose, substitute ½ teaspoon aspartame sweetener, or to taste.

◆

2 Servings, ³/₄ cup each

- 4 teaspoons unsweetened Dutch cocoa
- 2 large pinches cinnamon
- 1¼ cups double-strength coffee, divided
- 4 teaspoons fructose
- 3 tablespoons fat-free Kahlua-flavored non-dairy creamer
- 2 large glasses filled with ice cubes

P lace cocoa in small bowl and add cinnamon and 4 teaspoons coffee. Stir with wire whisk until smooth. Add remaining coffee, fructose, and Kahlua-flavored creamer. Stir again.
Divide between two ice-filled glasses.

◆

Nutritional Data

PER SERVING		EXCHANGES	
Calories:	73	Milk:	0.0
% Calories from fat:	4	Veg.:	0.0
Fat (gm):	0.3	Fruit:	0.0
Sat. fat (gm):	0.5	Bread:	1.0
Cholesterol (mg):	0	Meat:	0.0
Sodium (mg):	8	Fat:	0.0
Protein (gm):	0.9		
Carbohydrate (gm):	18		

◆

Cocoa Vanilla Mix

This cocoa mix is simple to make. It can then be stored in the cupboard and used to make cocoa as desired.

45 Servings, 1 mug each

Cocoa Mix
1½ cups unsweetened Dutch cocoa
6 tablespoons aspartame sweetener
1 vanilla bean

Hot Cocoa
¾ cup skim milk
2 level teaspoons Cocoa Mix
½ marshmallow

To Make Mix: Combine cocoa and aspartame in small jar. Cut vanilla bean in thirds and bury in mix. Cover tightly and store on cupboard shelf to use as needed.

To Make 1 Mug Hot Cocoa: Heat ¾ cup skim milk in saucepan. Place 2 level teaspoons Cocoa Mix in bowl. Add 2 tablespoons hot milk to Cocoa Mix and stir with whisk to combine. Stir in remaining milk, mixing well.

Pour into mug. Top with a half marshmallow. Serve immediately.

Nutritional Data

PER SERVING		EXCHANGES	
Calories:	88	Milk:	1.0
% Calories from fat:	6	Veg.:	0.0
Fat (gm):	0.6	Fruit:	0.0
Sat. fat (gm):	0.3	Bread:	0.0
Cholesterol (mg):	3	Meat:	0.0
Sodium (mg):	98	Fat:	0.0
Protein (gm):	8		
Carbohydrate (gm):	13		

INDEX